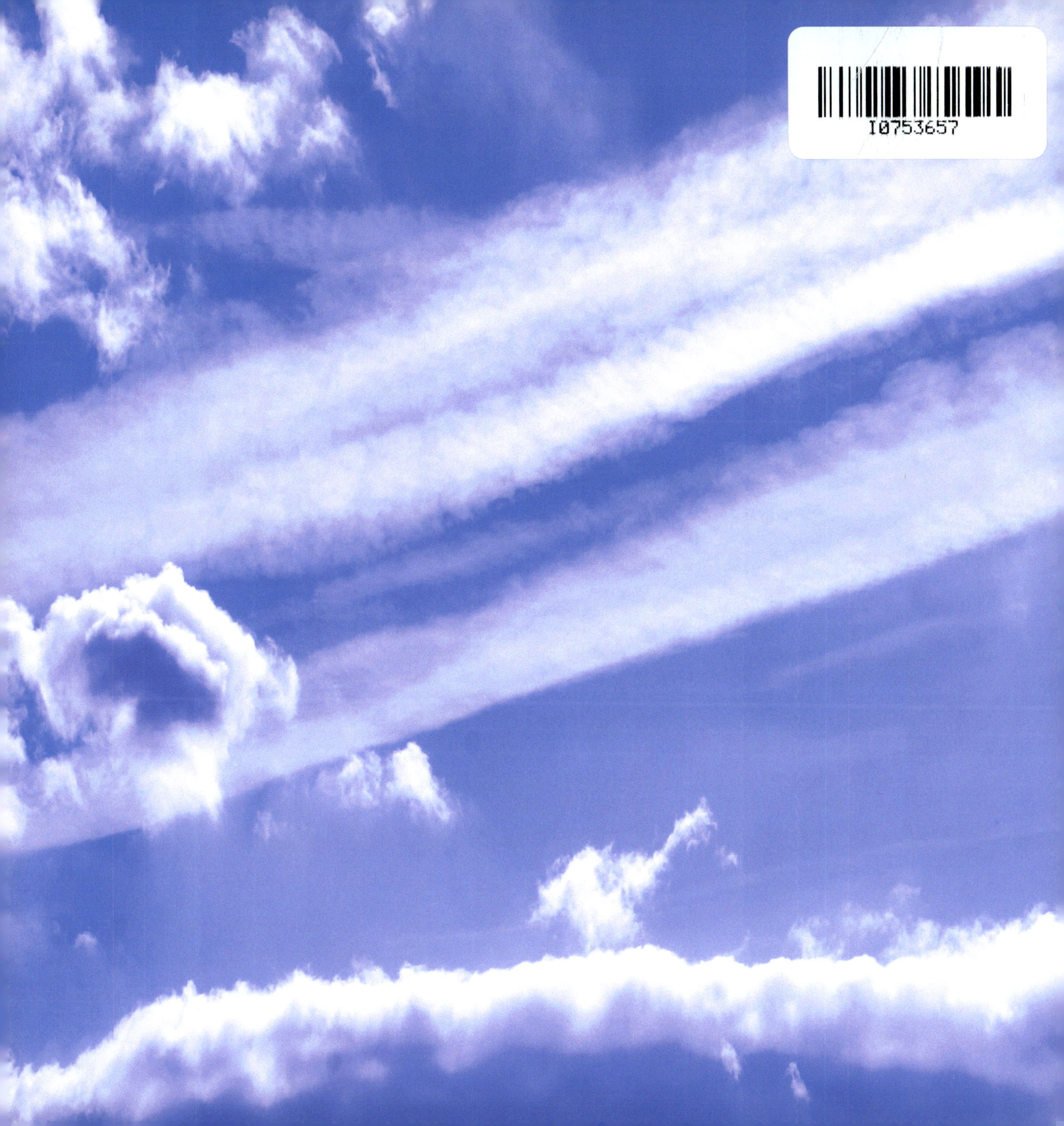
I0753657

HEAVEN & EARTH - Paradise et La Terre

Premier Edition Published in 2015 in the United States of America

*pg. 37 – Hills I Mourn [adapted] (1940's WWII) Willis Dean Couey (poem gifted to his mother, Emma L. Laughinghouse Knox.)

WWW.MYDOVESONG.COM

ISBN-13: 978-0692022047
ISBN-10: 069202204X

Heaven & Earth

PARADISE ET LA TERRE

D. ASHANTI-DUBOIS

My Dove Song
MYDOVESONG
PUBLISHING

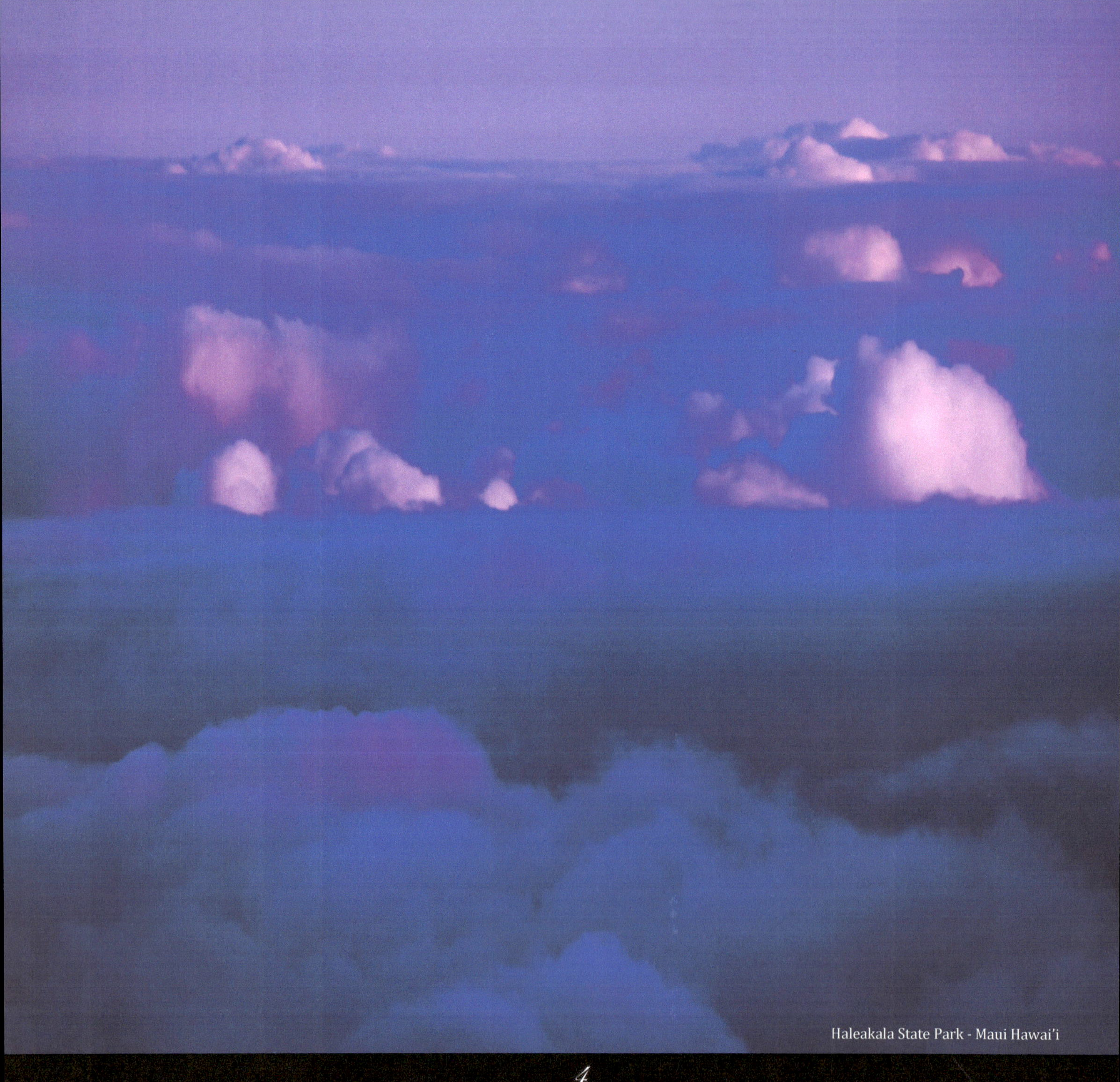

Haleakala State Park - Maui Hawai'i

Arise and rejoice, for tomorrow may never come. Seize this moment; see the heavens among the clouds. Live to the fullest and embrace the waking dawn. Partake of the joys that life can bestow. Be it rain or shine, sleet or storm, open your heart and free your soul, for a time will come when the shadows fall. Let you spirit will dance decadently against the wall and live, before this day is done...

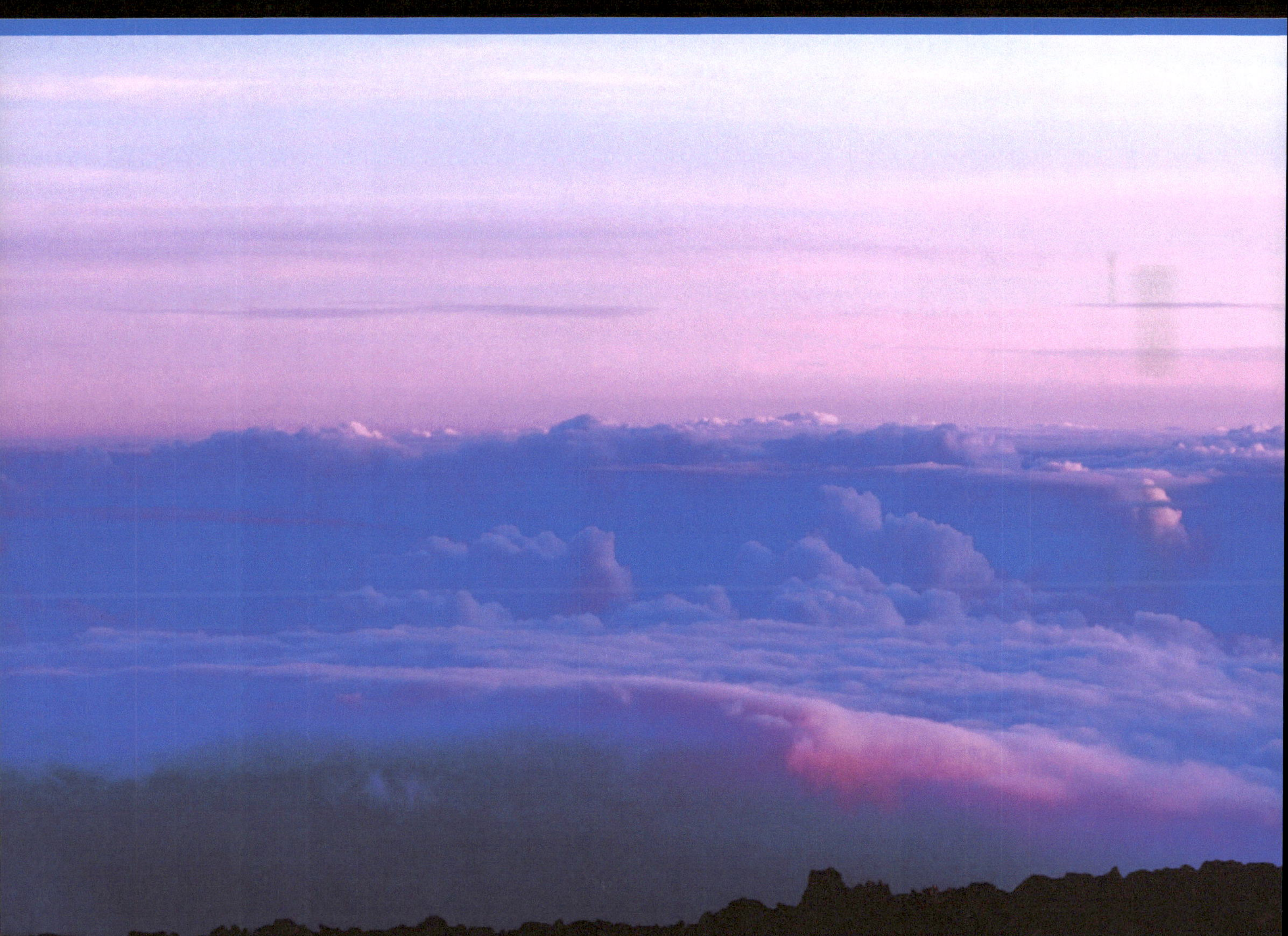

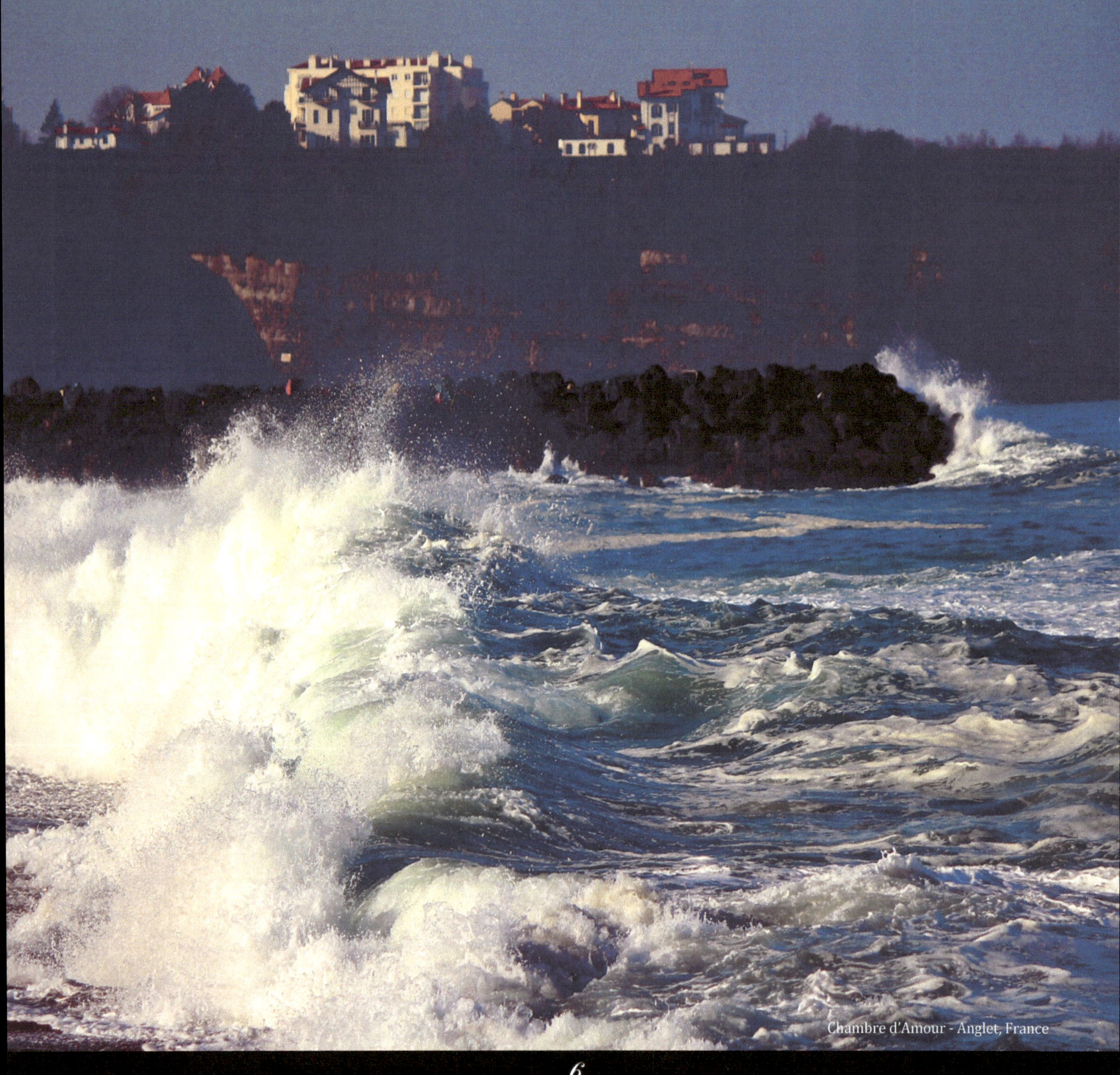

Chambre d'Amour - Anglet, France

Run like the waves across the ocean floor. Feel the tiny pebbles beneath your feet teeming with life and smooth to the touch. Love like the mountains, bold and courageously pure. Stand firm and do not waver on what you know will endure, yet live like the heavens, open, and full of joy. Life is the epitome of nature; so beautiful, magical, and more precious than words...yet as fragile as the wings of a dove.

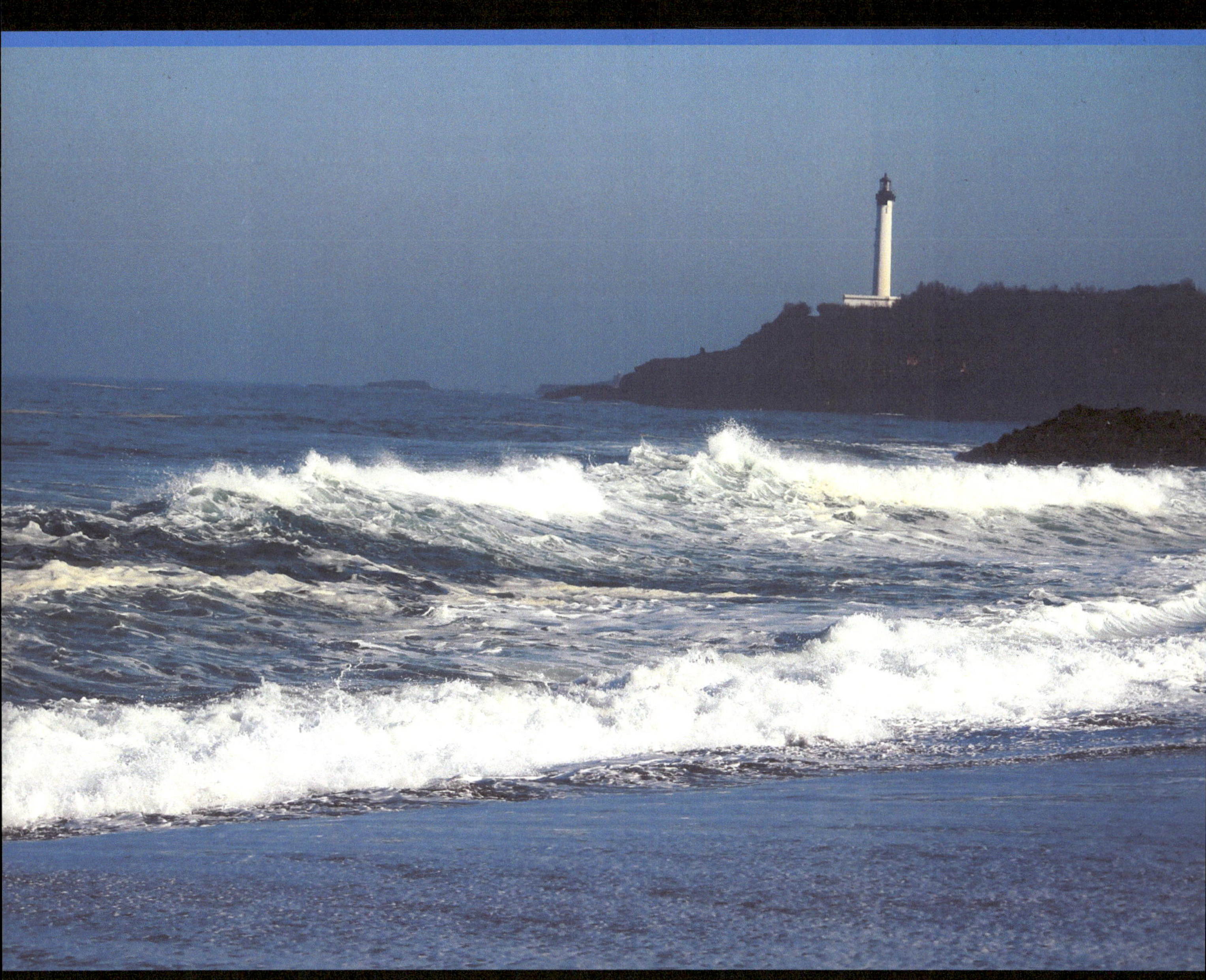

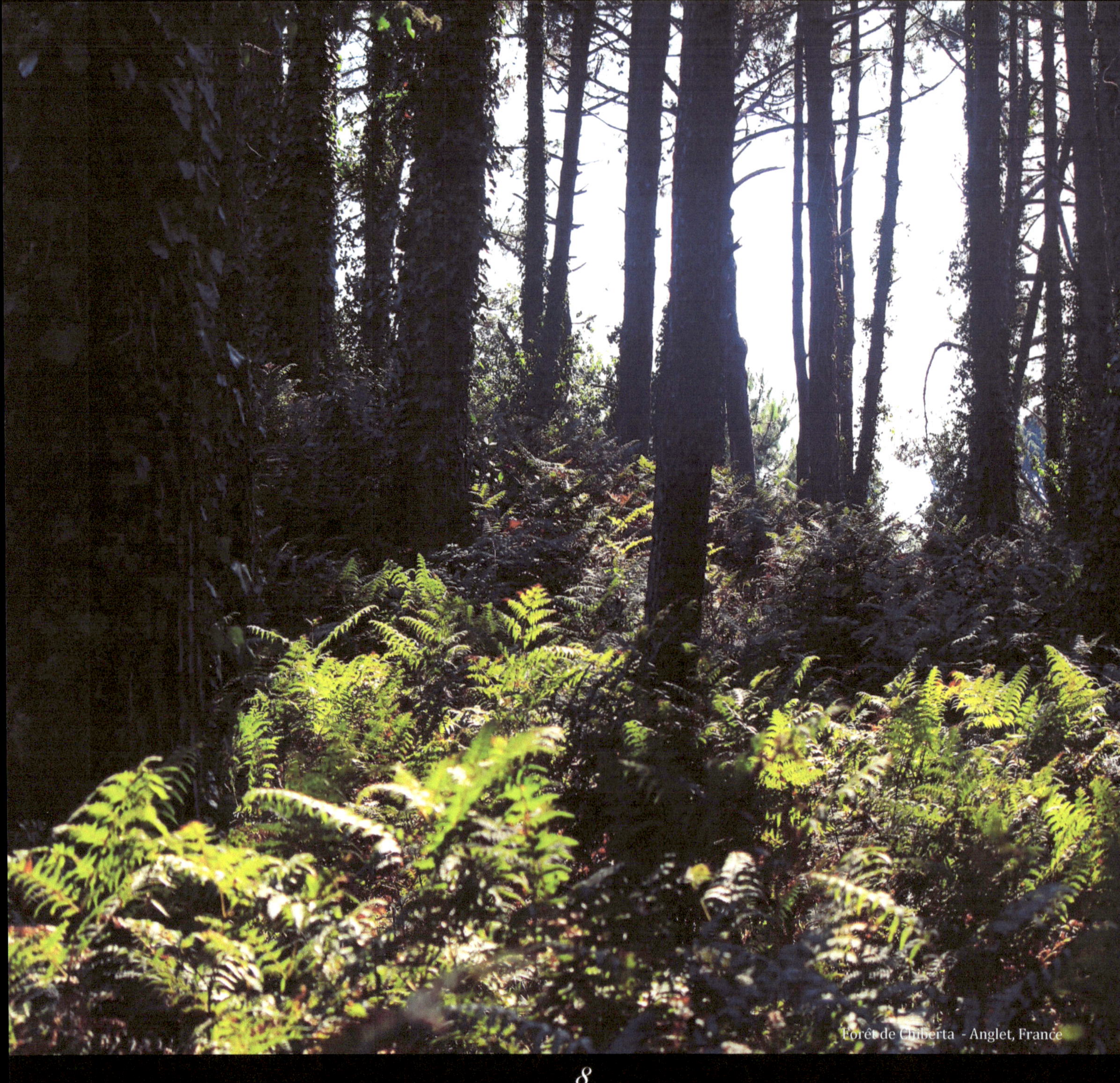

Forêt de Chiberta - Anglet, France

Morning peers incandescently through the branches of the trees, as leaves tumble aimlessly to the ground. Birds fly from nest to nest, as the flow of the river shimmers in the light of nature's fragrant scent. Feel alive in the midst of peace; wander free through time. Lean back and relax your mind. Breathe in peace and be refreshed. Life among the trees has no worries; what a gift of pure happiness...

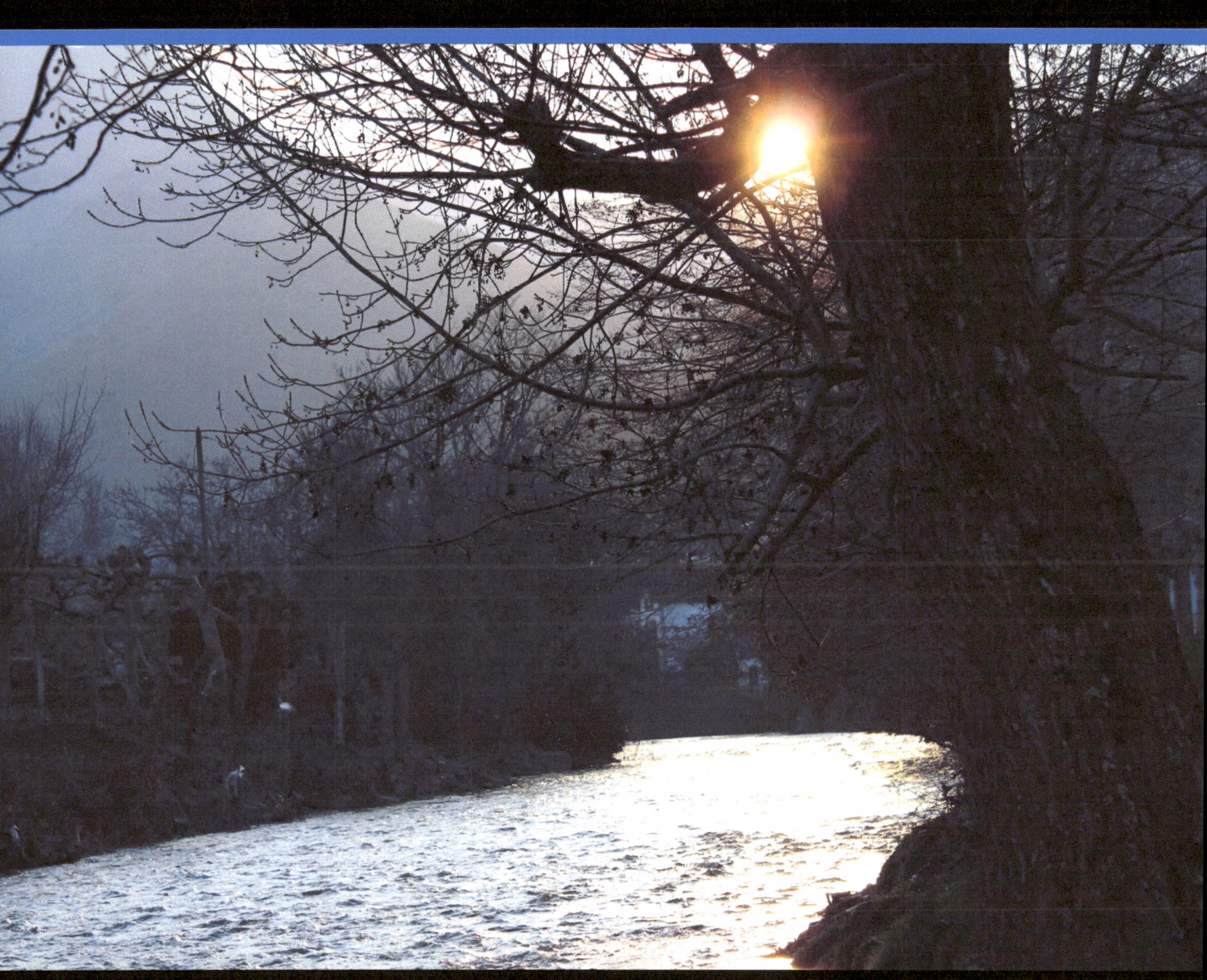

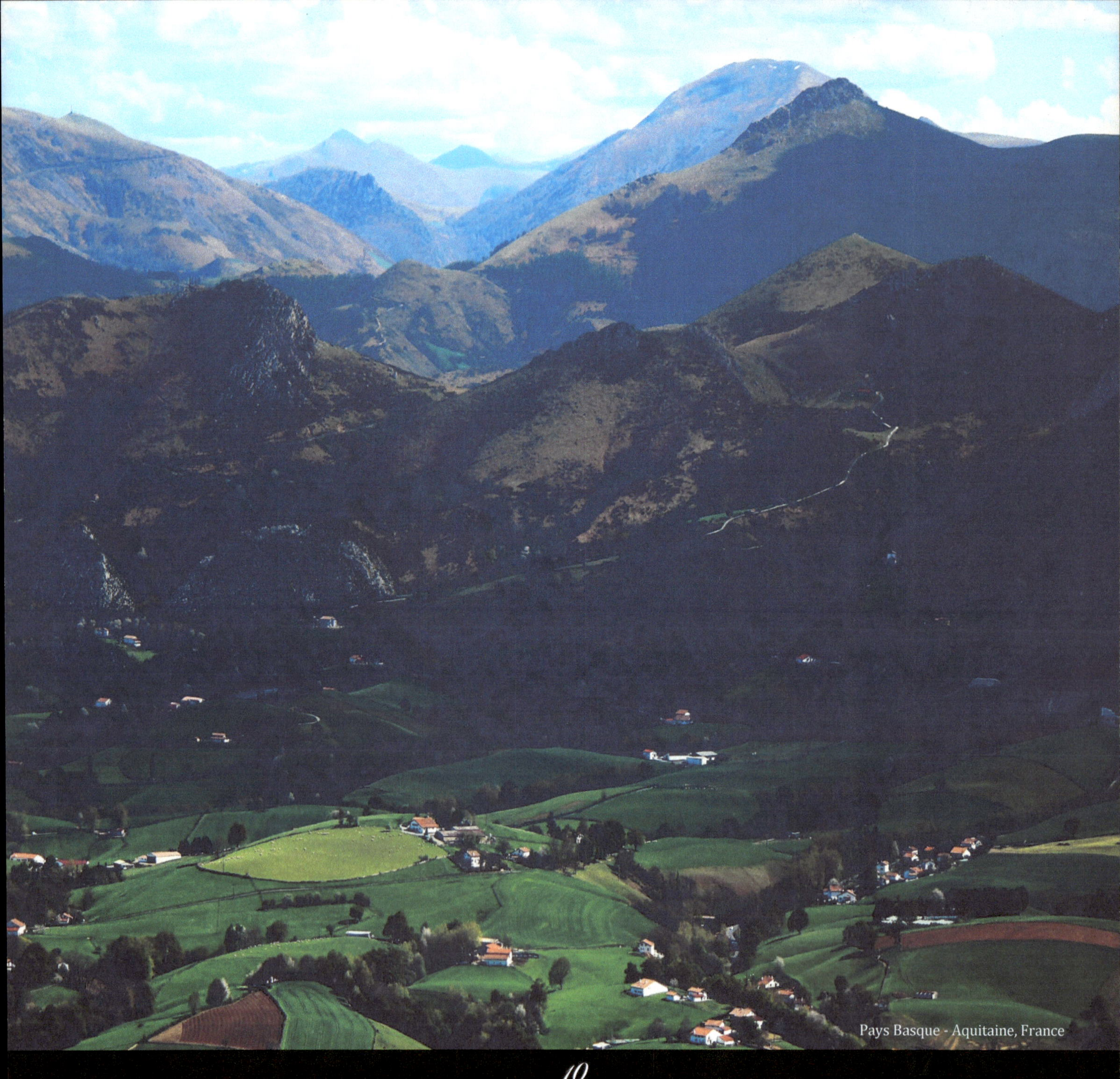

Pays Basque - Aquitaine, France

The earth is full of beautiful things...things that money cannot buy. Your thoughts are worth more than mere diamonds; they are the riches of your mind. In the simplicity of life, wisdom and clarity awaits you. When the clutter of indecision disappears, the renewed hope of joy enters in. Whether in a rich and vibrant meadow or the park up the hill, let your spirit roam free and live...

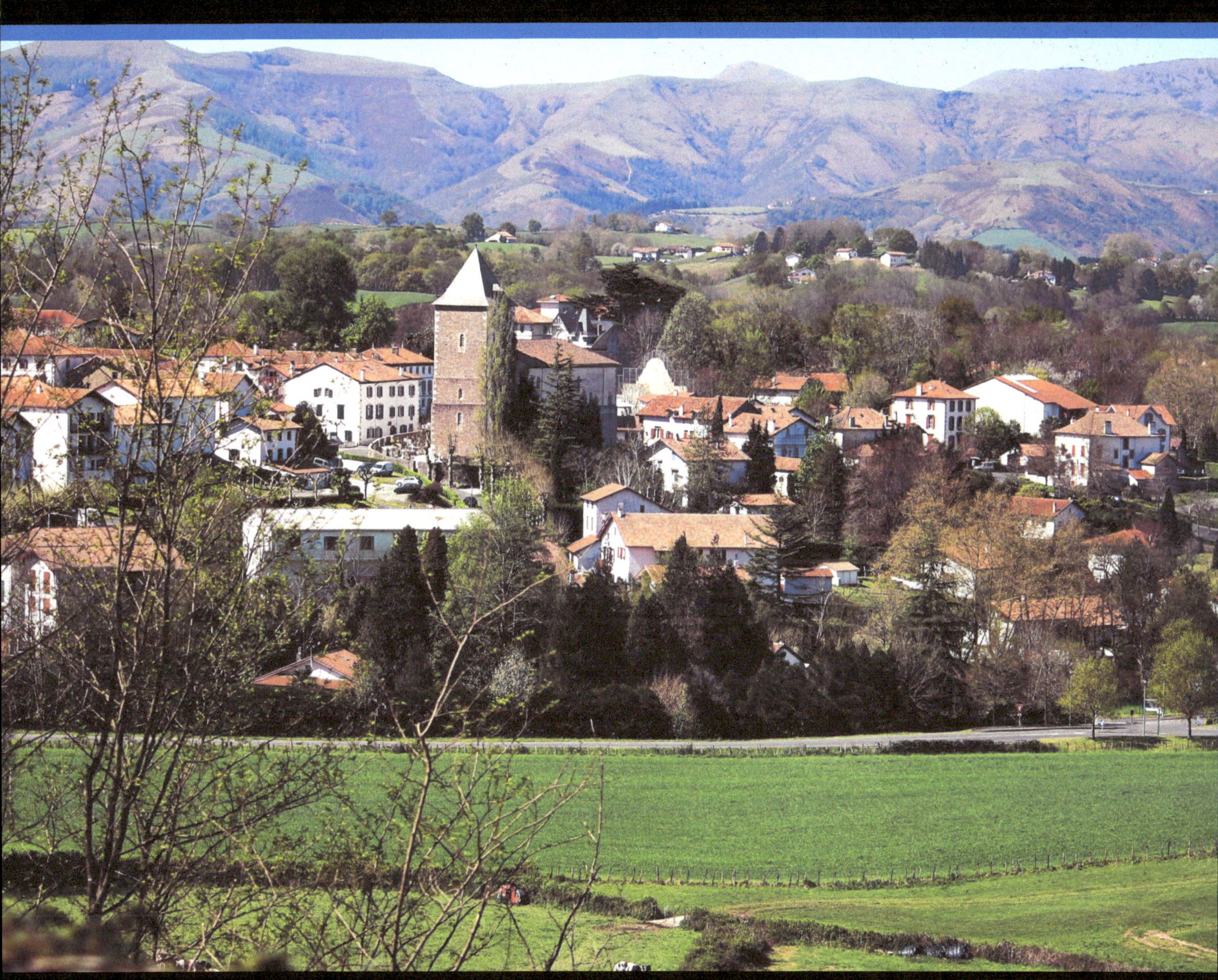

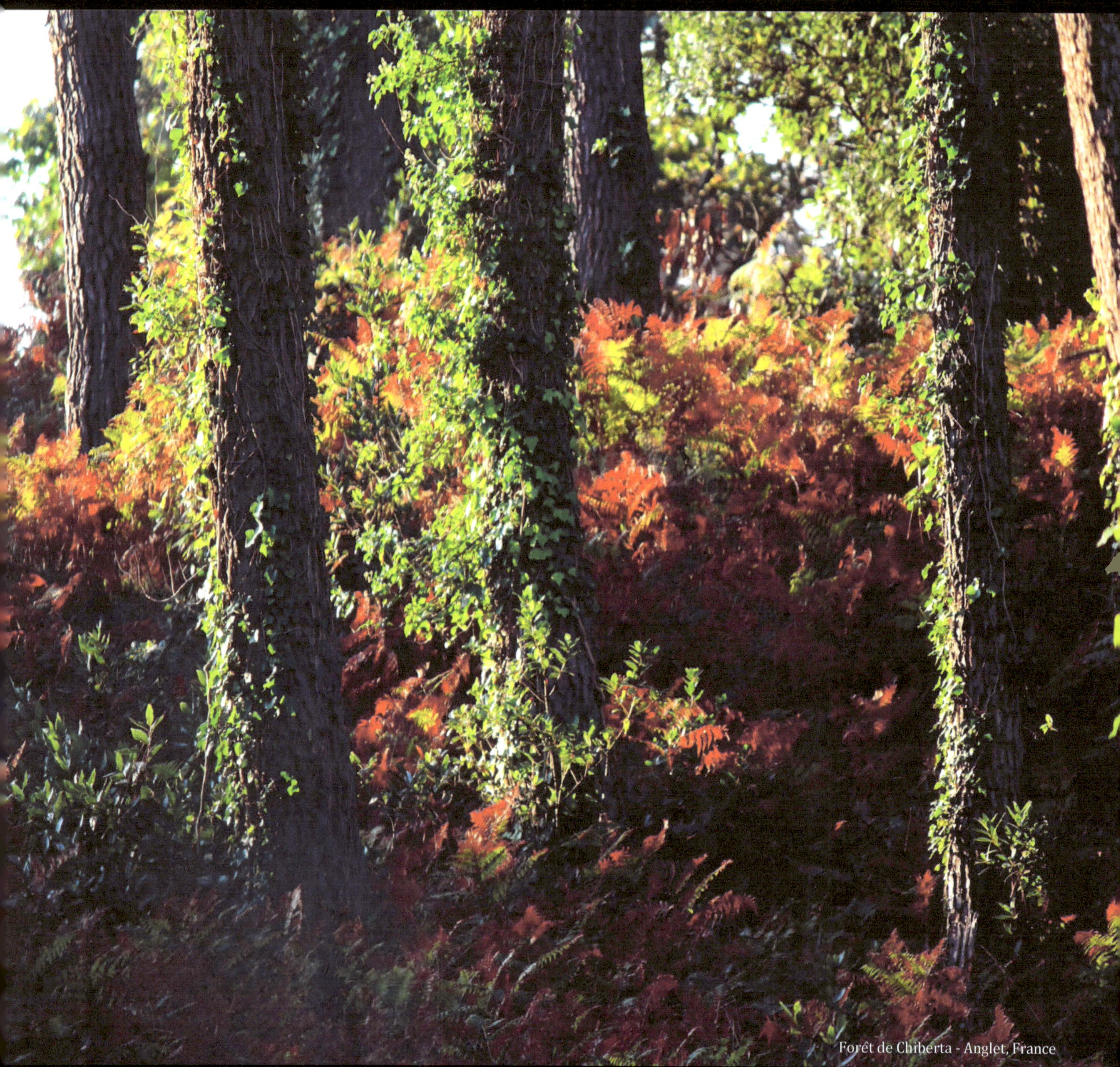

Forêt de Chiberta - Anglet, France

Early in the morning when the sun joins the sky, an arbor sits in a field wondering how time went by. Once you swung on it's branches and carved out your name. Once you rested against it's sturdy bark and played hide and seek behind it's frame. Harken back to the time when you were young and free. Return to that joy; return to that tree. There you will discover the child who rests in you.

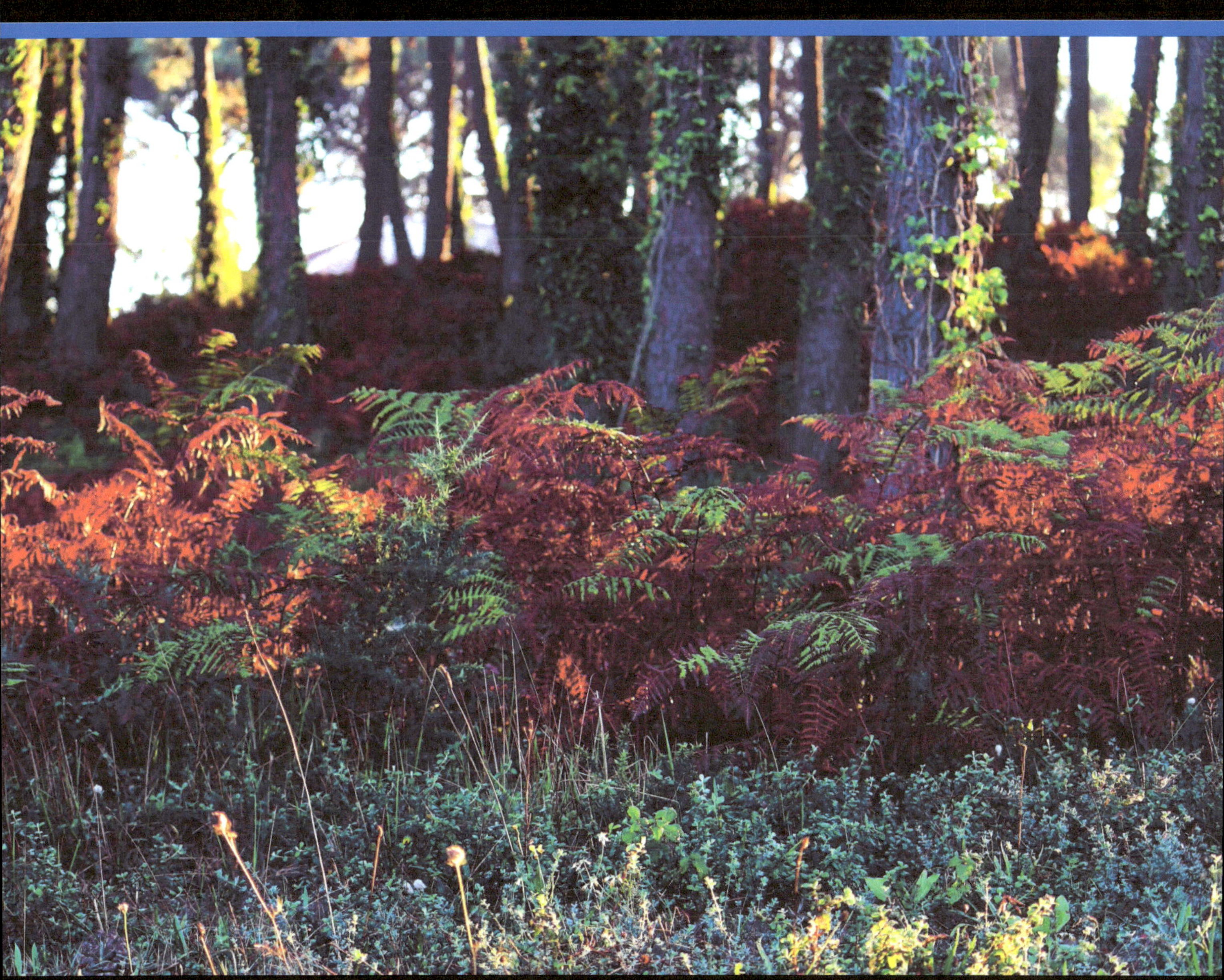

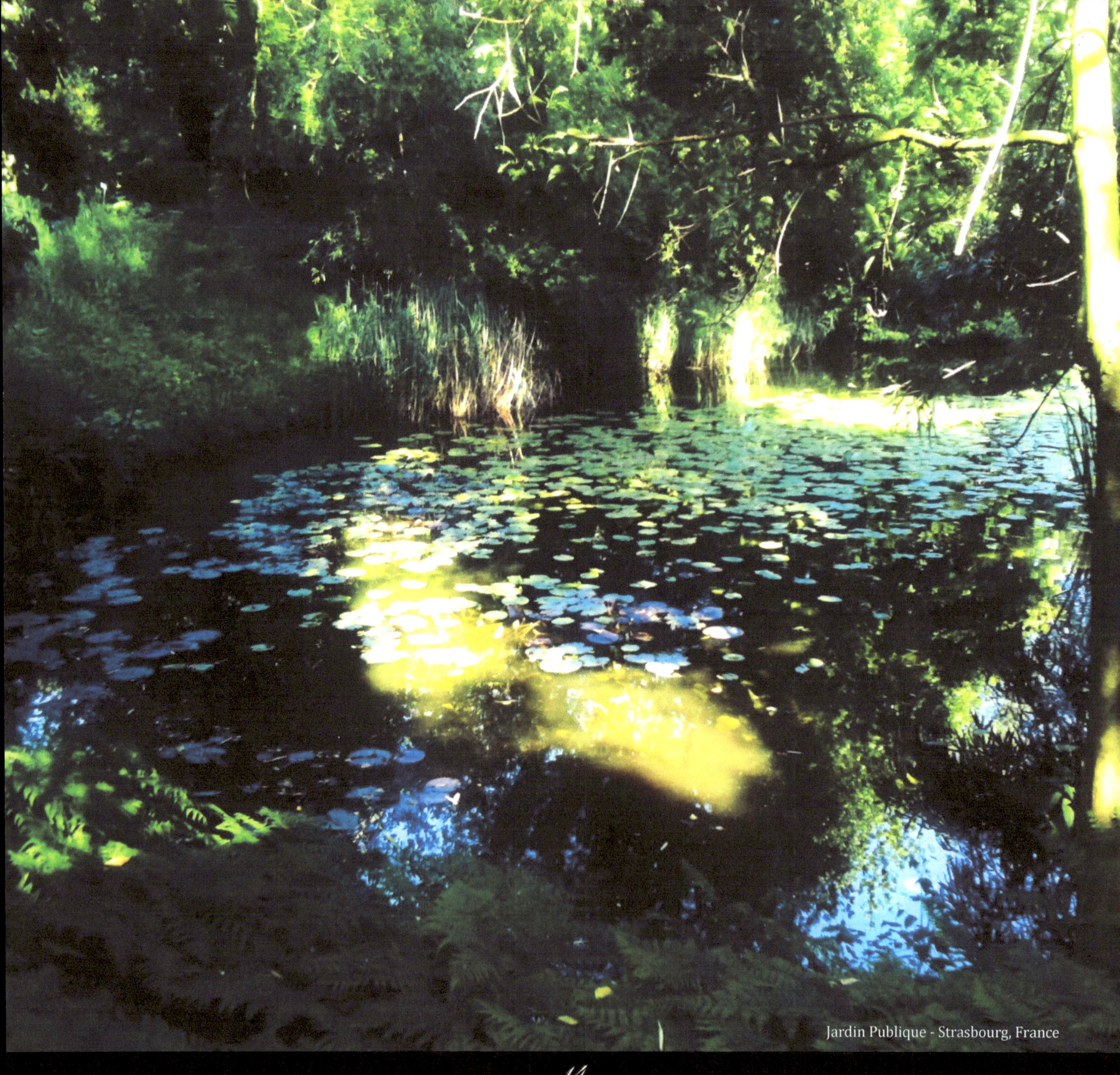

Jardin Publique - Strasbourg, France

Enjoy the fruits of your labor. Give yourself the gift of time. Time spent laughing, loving, eating the fruit you've gathered. For this earth you tarried not, and yet she is yours for the taking. So, kick off your shoes, relax your mind. Feel the sun against your skin. Slid your hand over a flower, touch a leaf, or smell sweet jasmine. The earth is a gift you can never earn, and yet, she freely gives...

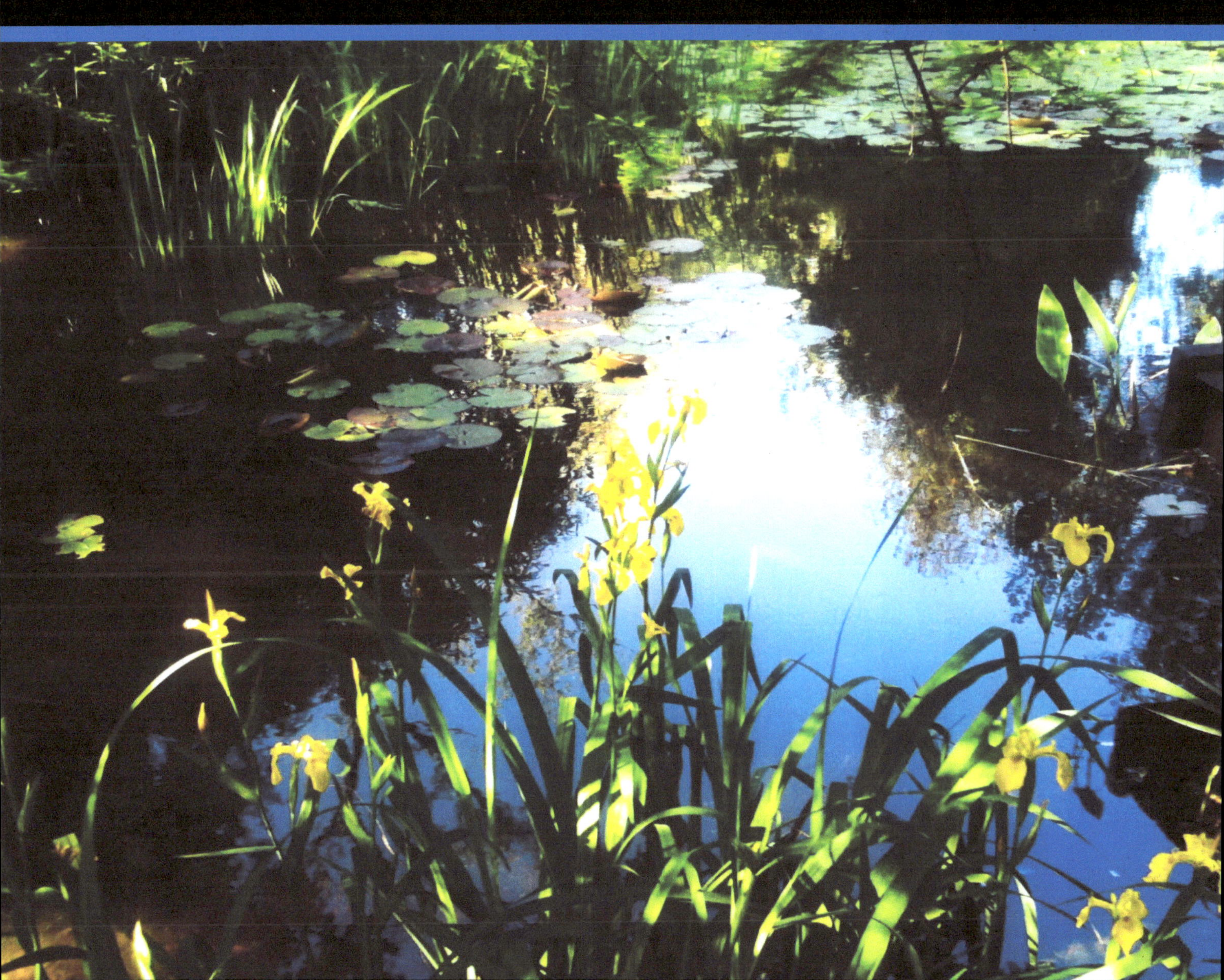

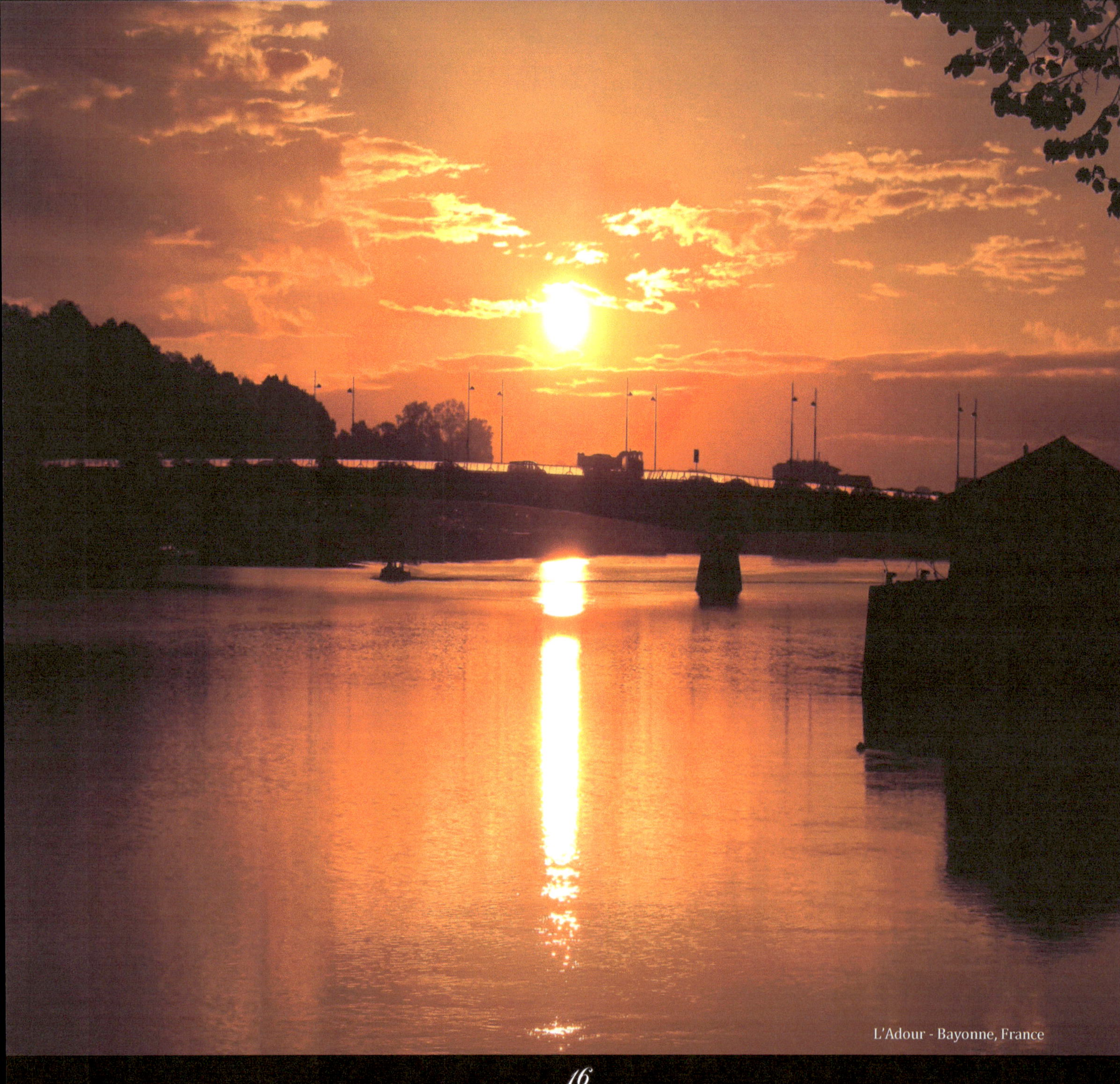

L'Adour - Bayonne, France

The sun beams down on a bridge to heaven and caresses the river's smiling face. You stop and look back to see how far you've come.
You ponder your chosen fate wondering which path ought to take. The journey ahead is a mystery, yet the path behind you is gone.
Keep walking towards your destiny, for soon the nightfall will come. A life that is not truly lived is like a river that cannot run.

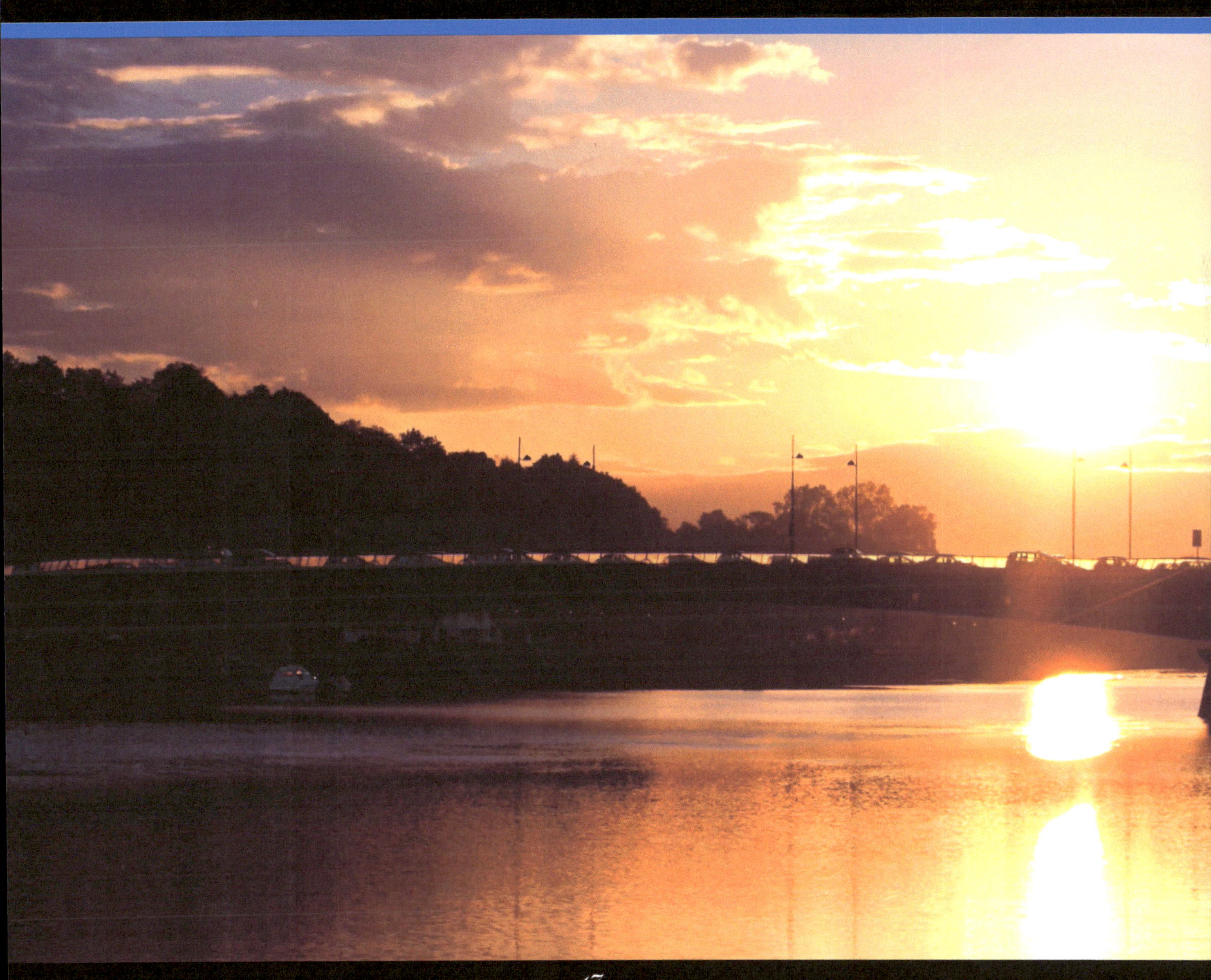

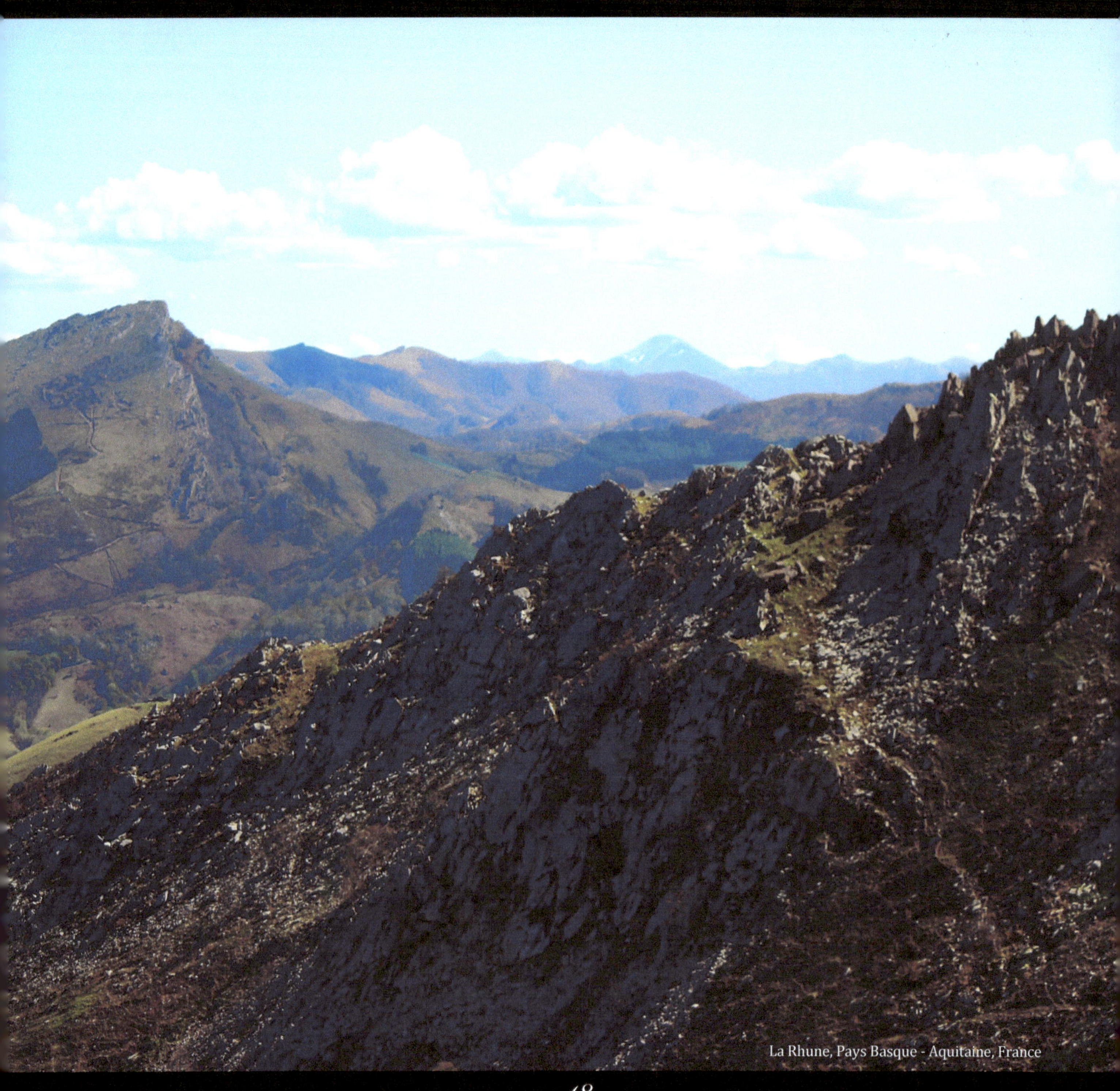
La Rhune, Pays Basque - Aquitaine, France

Here I stand on the top of a mountain, overwhelmed by the beauty of the land. I arrived by the hard road and am truly blessed to be alive. I look over the canyons beyond the horizon below. I sense a quiet storm stirring inside my soul. Like the gentle rain, tears begin to flow. I am not sad; I rejoice instead. I survived the worst and I live to tell the tale. Each scar of my life is a mountain overcome.

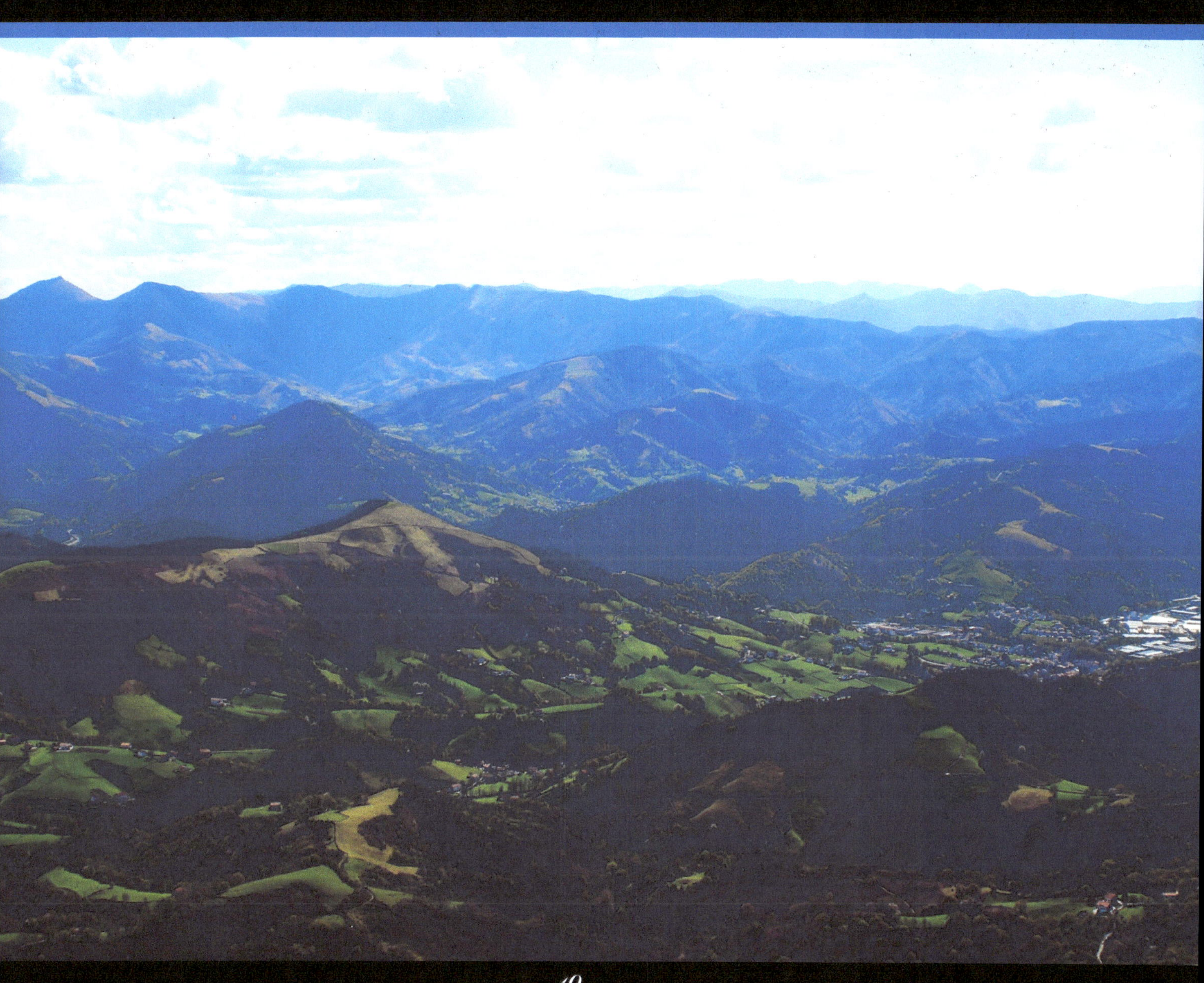

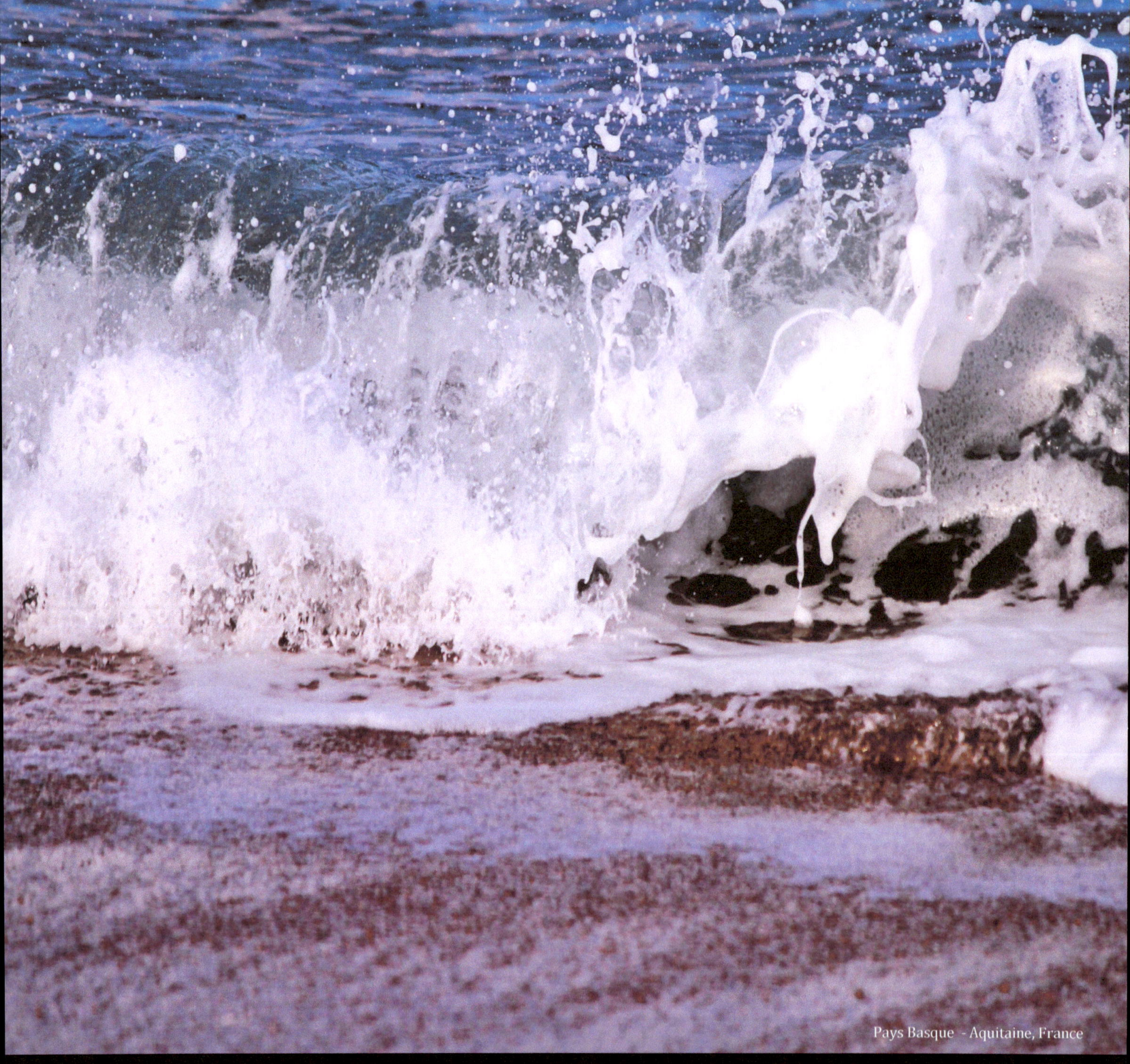
Pays Basque - Aquitaine, France

Love is like the waves splashing upon the shore. It ebbs and flows...advances and recedes. Life on earth is good, yet it changes like the wind... You are up and you are down. We are ruled by the moon; yet desirous of the sun. Winter comes and autumn goes... We dream of right and awake to wrong. The sky looks down upon us, yet reflects the heavens above. We are like the waves; ruled by love.

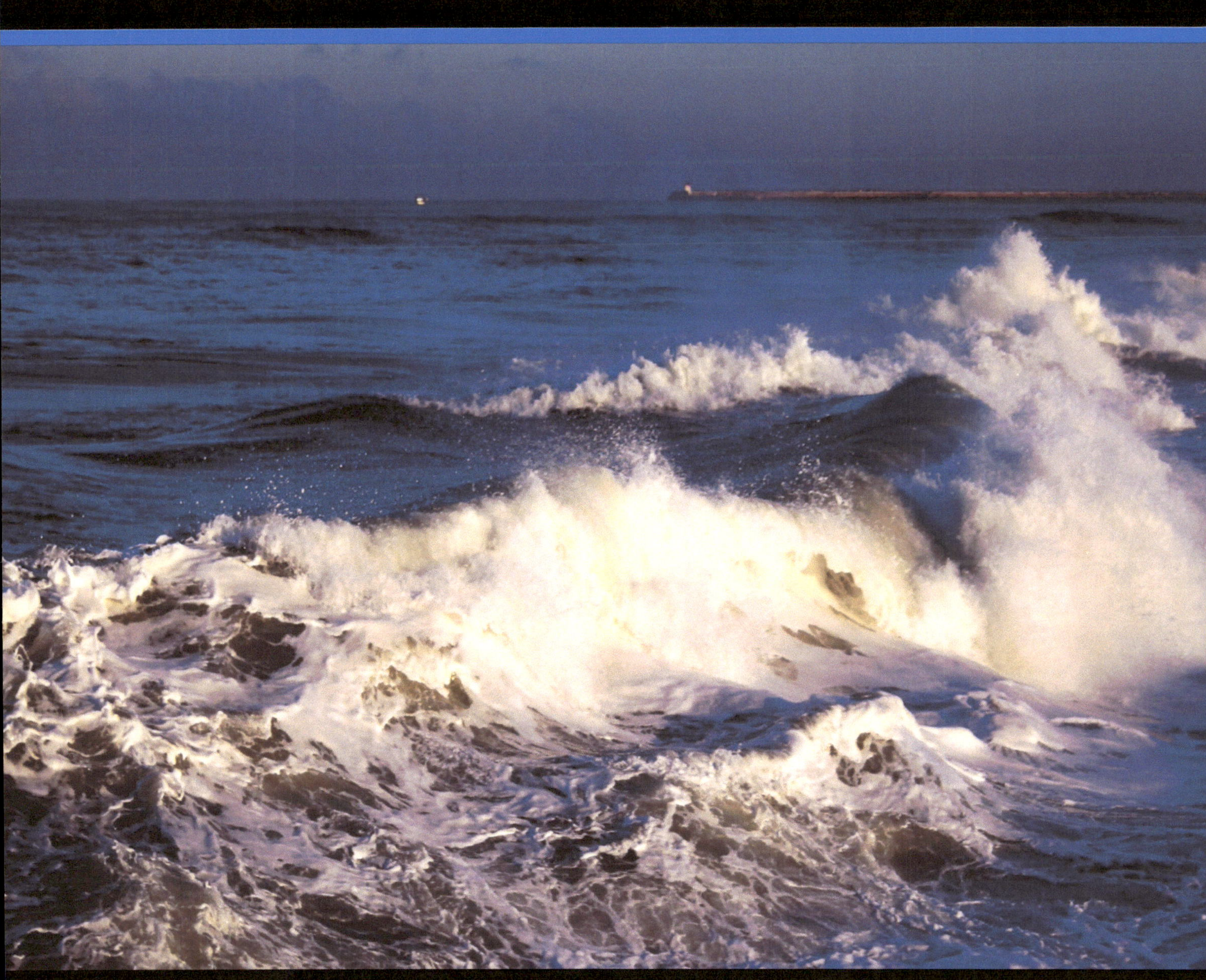

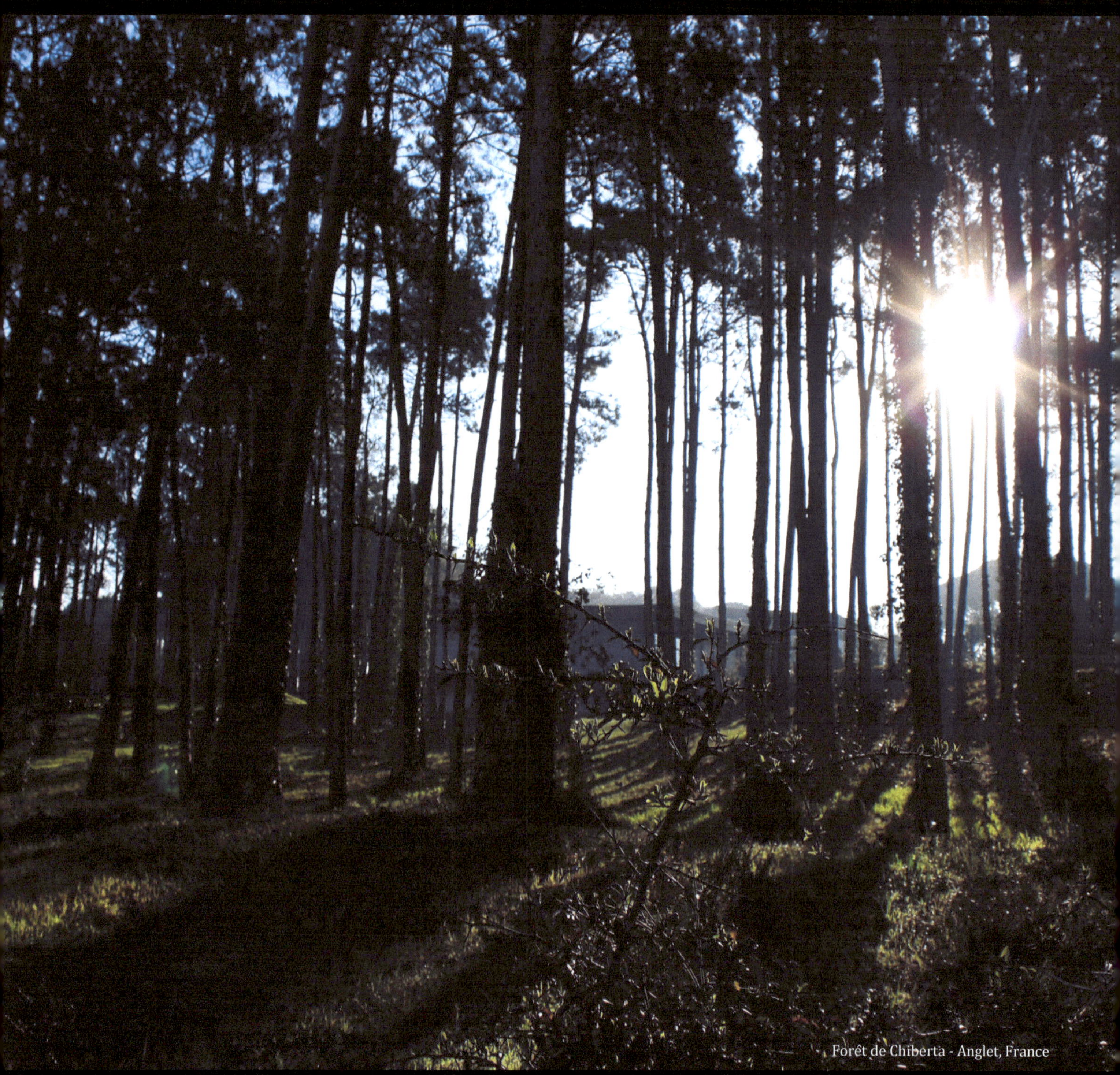

Forêt de Chiberta - Anglet, France

Be as strong as the aspen, rugged as the oak, and as fierce t as the pine. Live like the mulberry bushes growing wildly uninhibited across the leafy ferns. There is nothing you cannot be and nothing you cannot do. Plant your seed deep and you will grow strong. You are a redwood, maple, a bamboo, or a mighty ash. You exist in an imperfect world, infinitely blessed by a perfect earth.

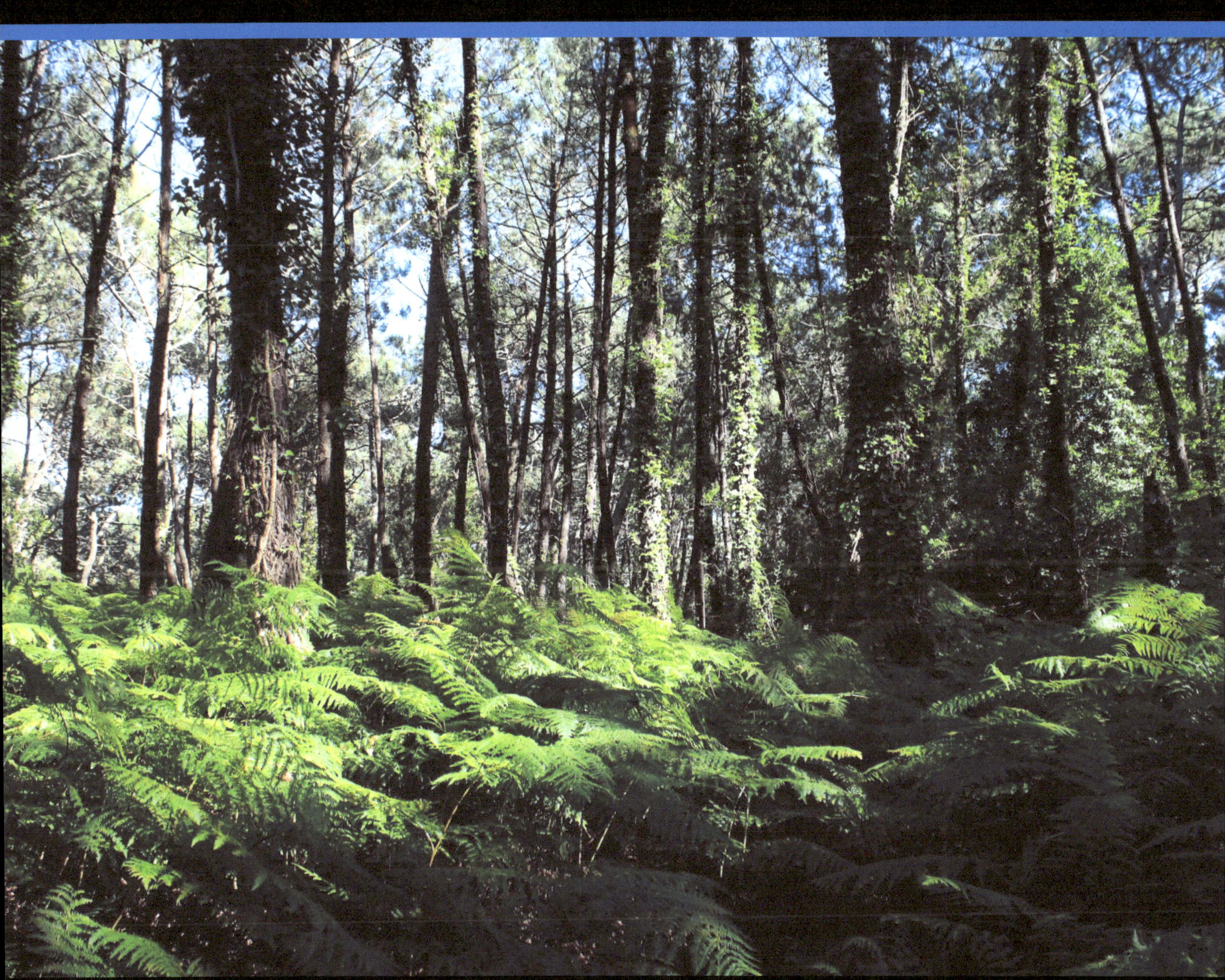

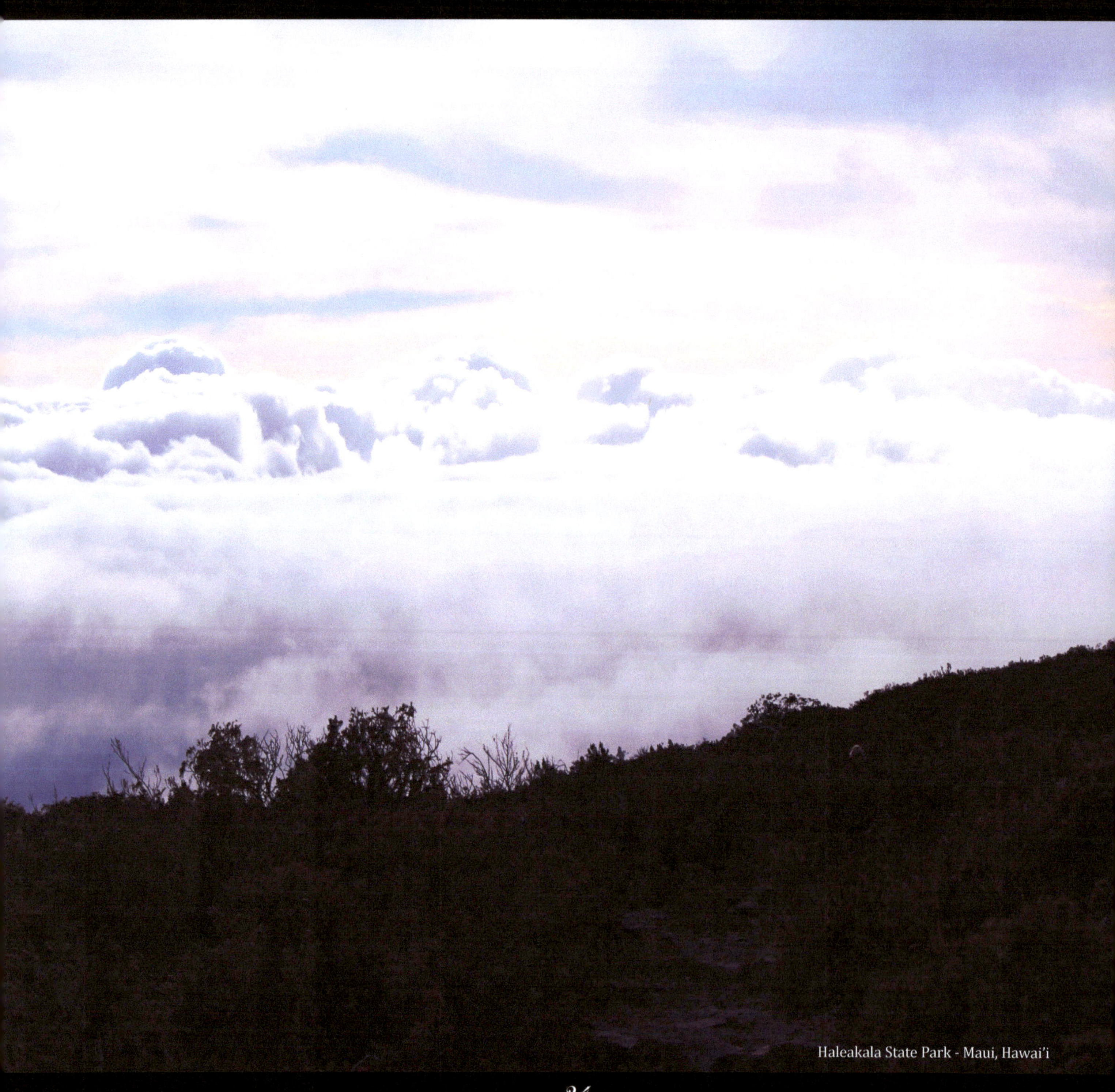

Haleakala State Park - Maui, Hawai'i

The heavens surround you... The earth is below you... Reach out and touch the clouds. The air is pure and so is your desire. All your dreams were meant to come true. Make a wish; all of your desires are already waiting for you. Just step out on faith and destiny will catch you. Have no fear; live on top of the world. You were born for great things and great things are born from you...

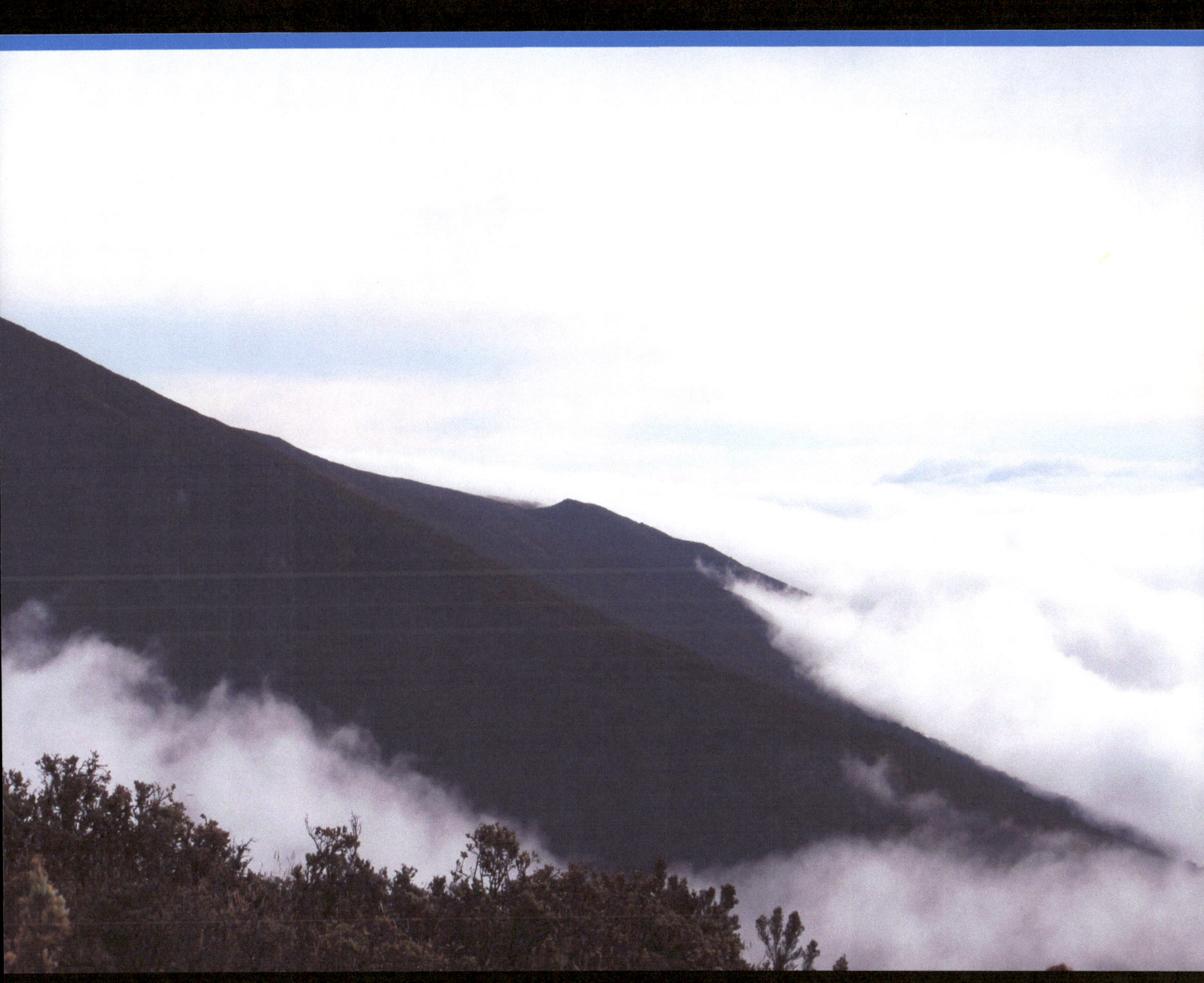

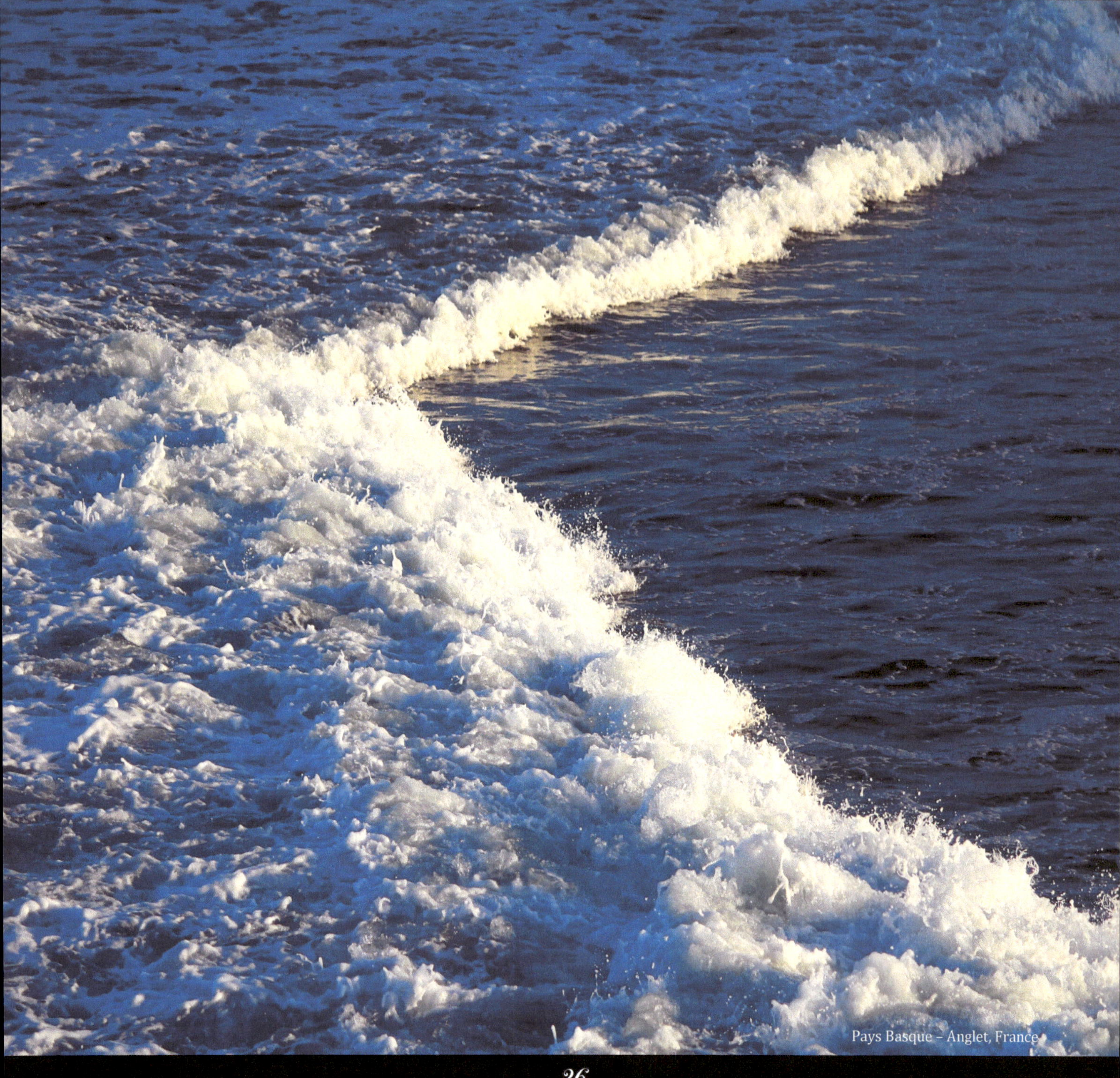

Pays Basque – Anglet, France

Shower your heart with laugher;drink of effervescent joy. We're in a race against time, so live it to the fullest. Dive into this illusion called life. Smile before your storm is over; rejoice before the victory is won. Relish in the power to rewrite your story and splurge in the imminence of now. Life is yours for the taking, so meander through it unafraid. Now go and take your chances before it's too late.

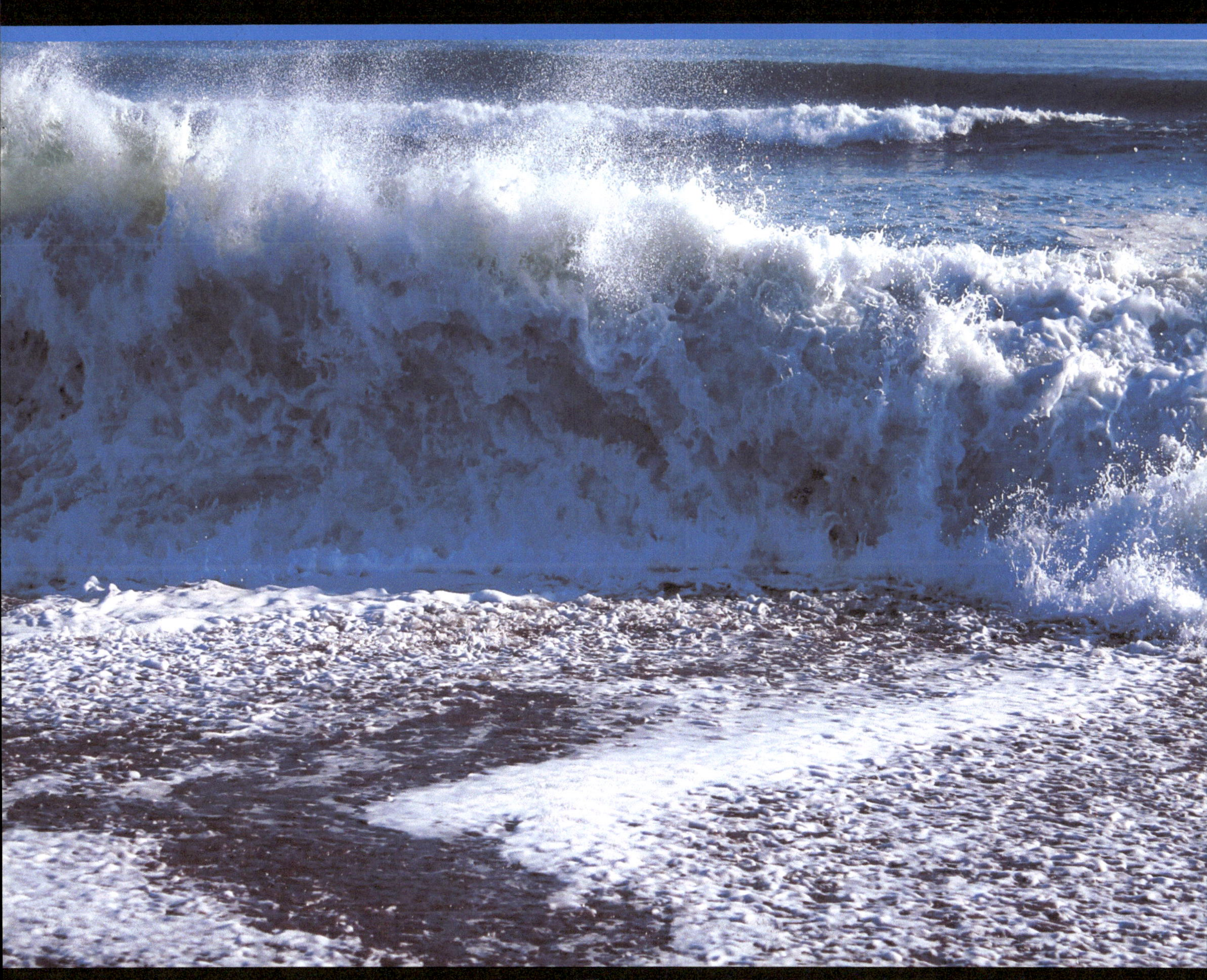

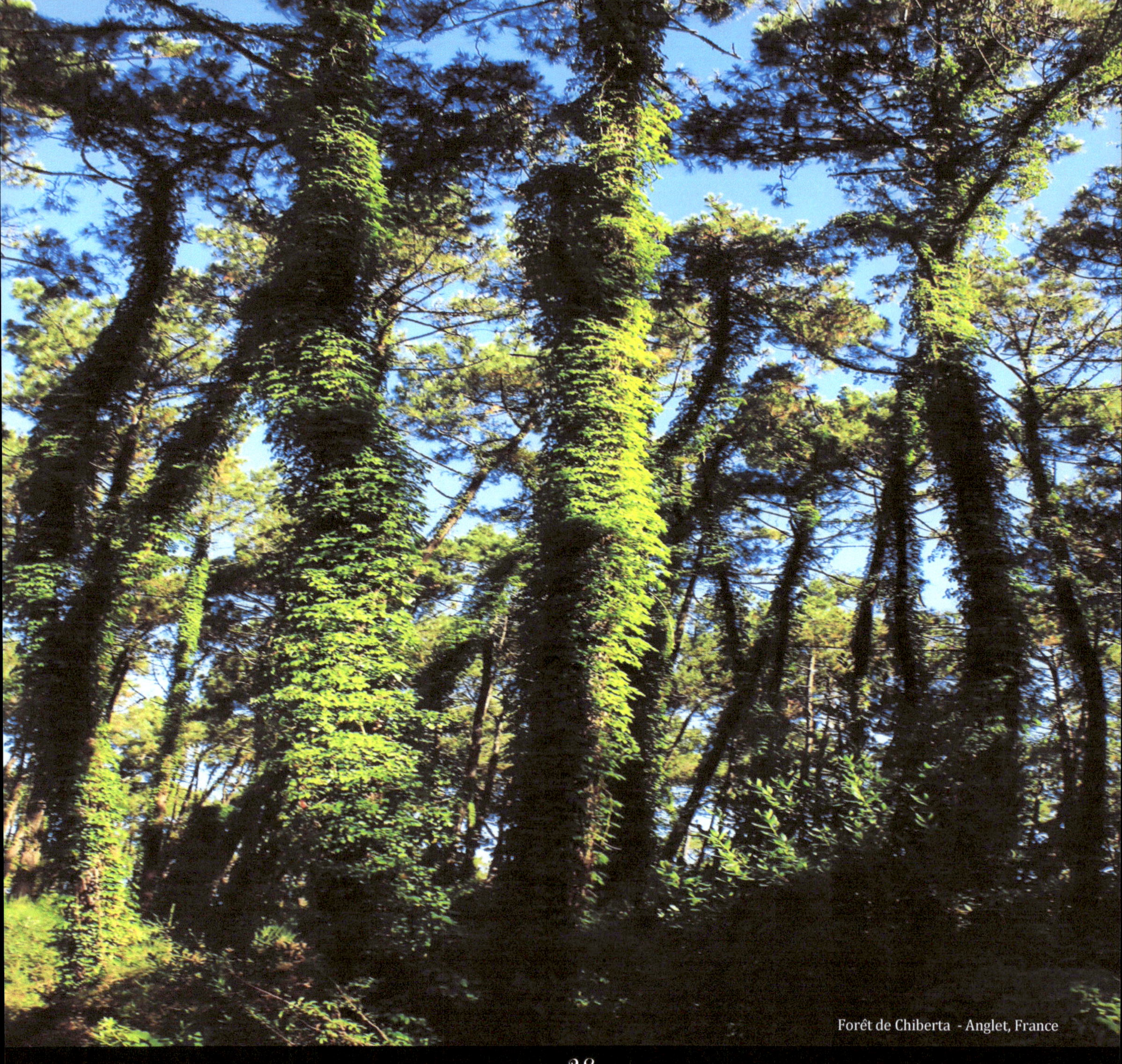
Forêt de Chiberta - Anglet, France

Wander beneath the majestic beams of nature's finest cache and partake of the treasure that cost you nothing, but is worth the entire universe. Lovely and peaceful glorious earth; such a bountiful treasure magnificent from birth. It's an astounding enclave of blue, green and gold...a lair so pristine like a rose bed of petals; a lush leafy grove far from man's eye... It's just a tickle of the beauty in paradise...

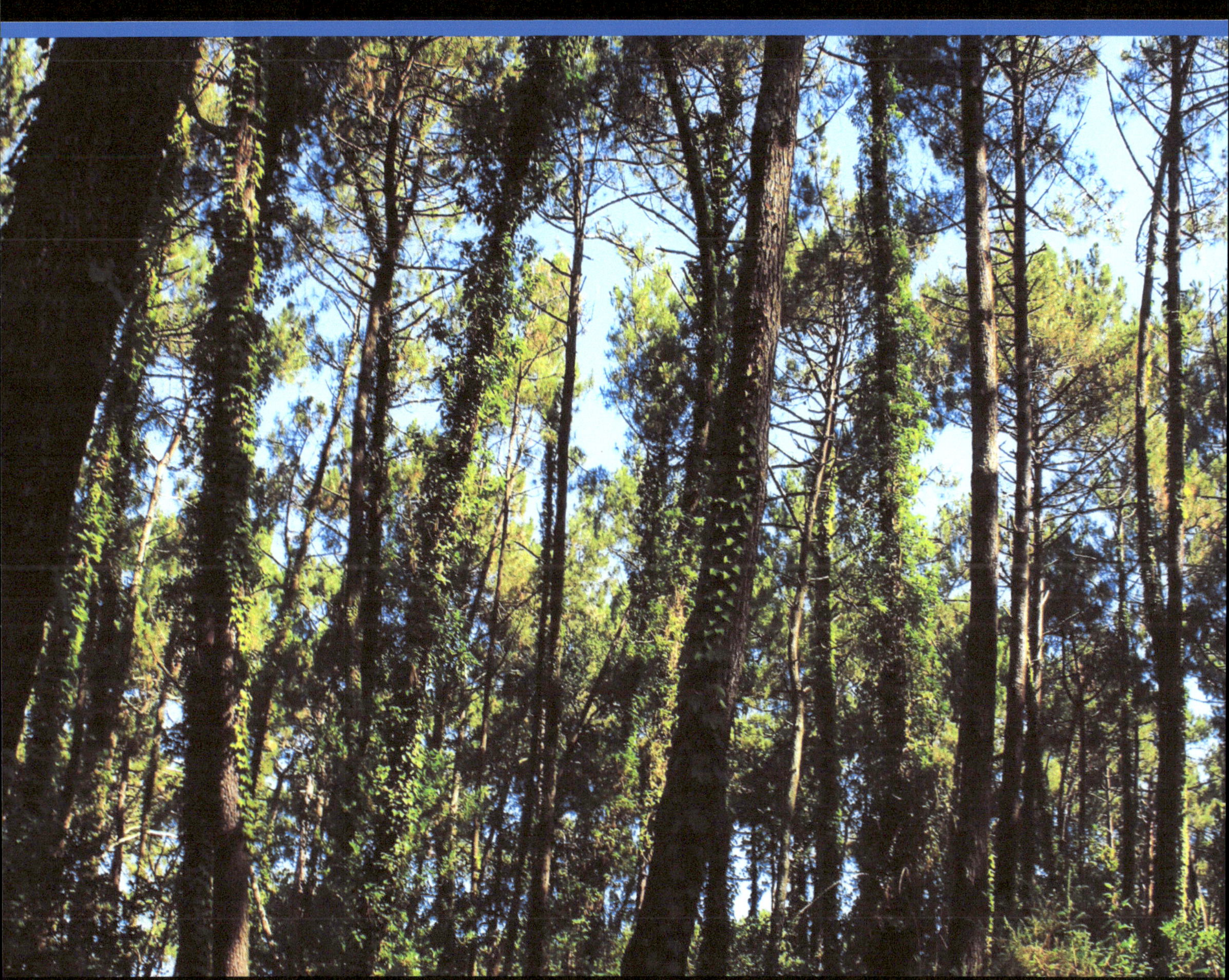

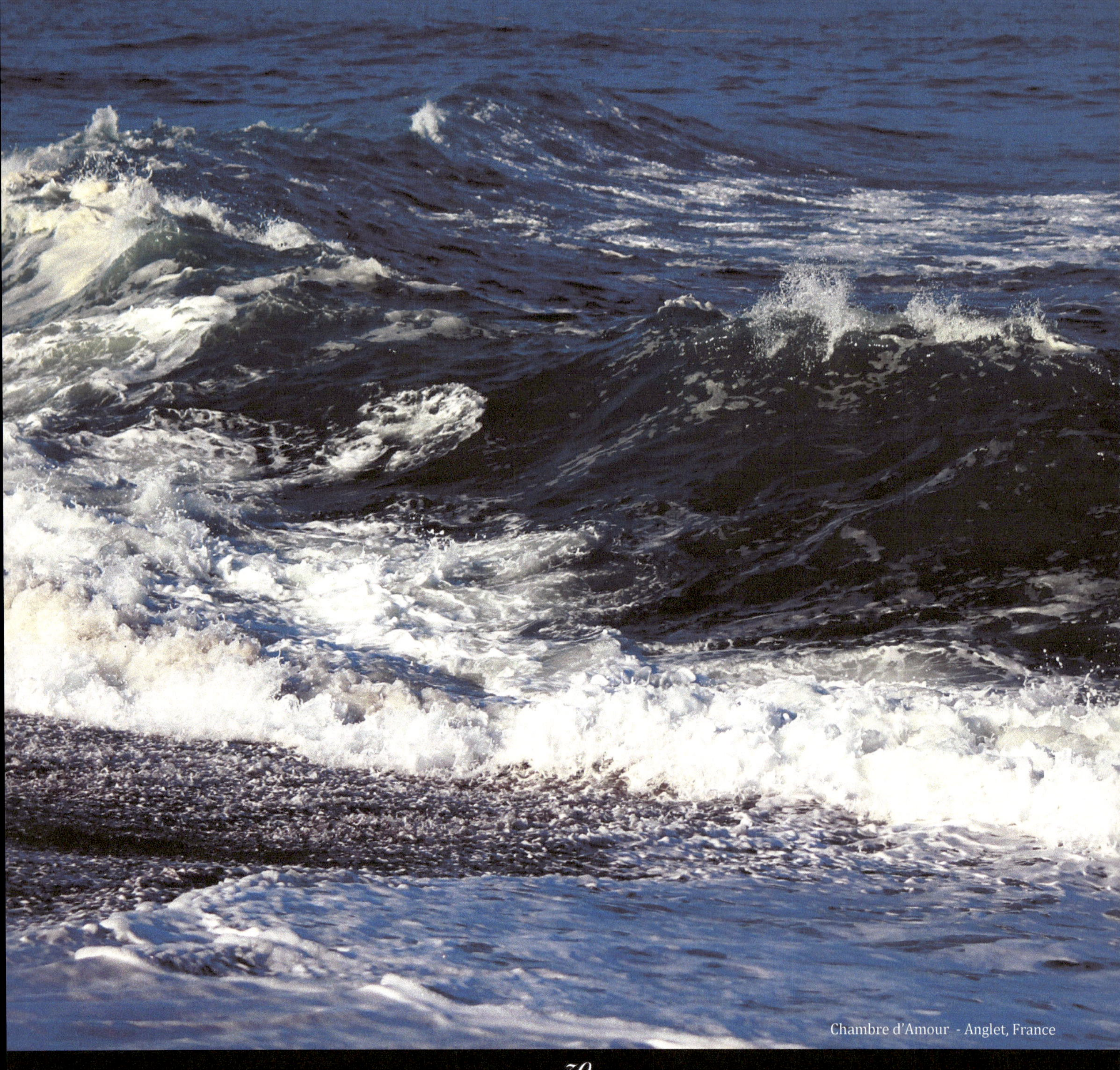
Chambre d'Amour - Anglet, France

Its power is born of the deep, a vitality that thrives. The ocean is like thunder; energy coming alive. Wind upon water, waves upon the sea, the wondrous white fury storms the sandy beach. Soft wet whipped cream swirling around your feet, awaking all your senses, yet lulling you into peace. Herein lies the meaning of life... Always be bold, daring, gentle, and alive...

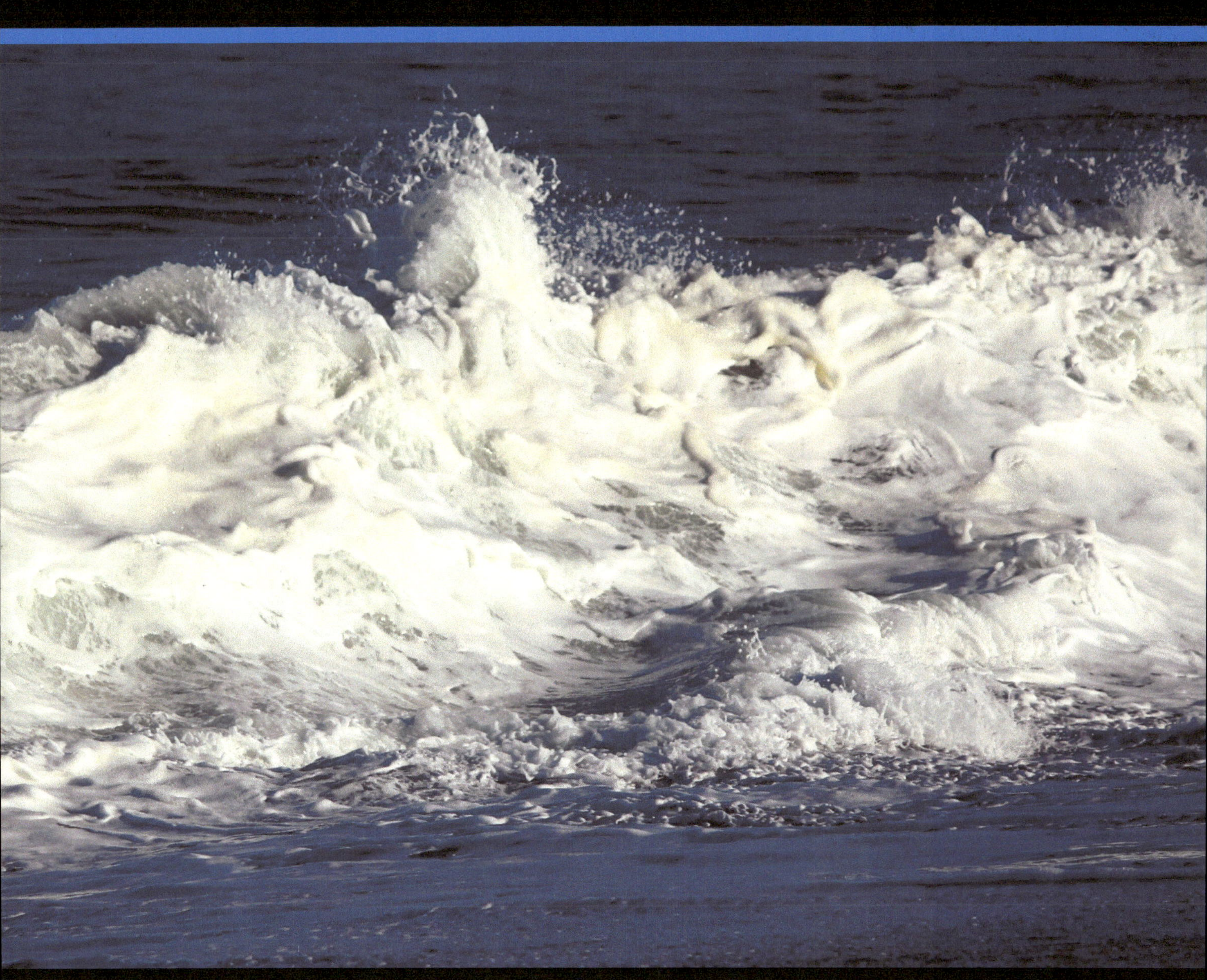

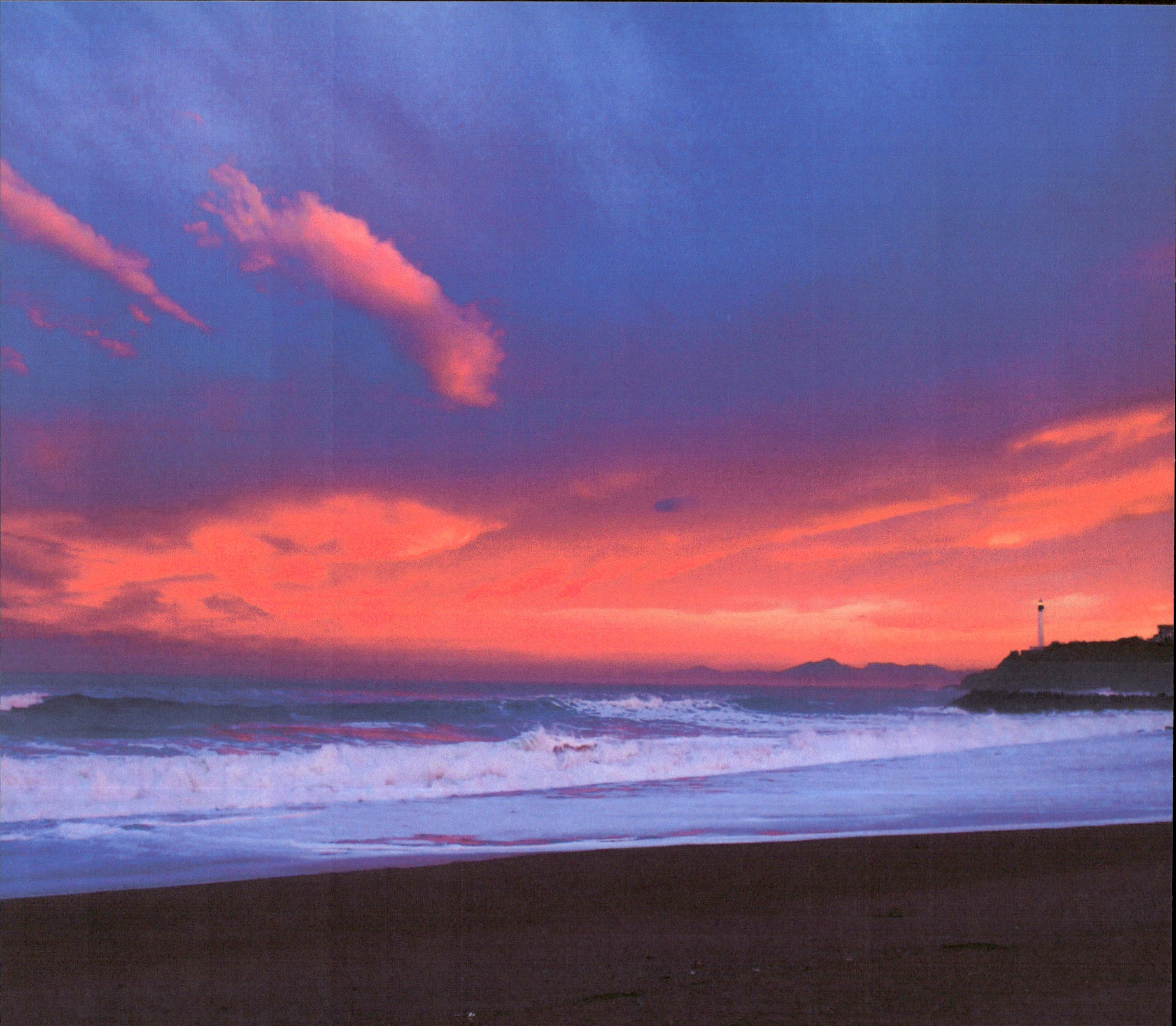

The morning breaks and the heavens open wide. Nothing holds you back and only hope stirs your mind. The skies are glowing in rich vibrant hues, the water is healing, and the earth is your muse. Take a walk along the seashore and reminisce about what you hold dear. All is possible between heaven and earth; just dream, hope, and believe, and never ever fear... Make what you dream; destiny is near...

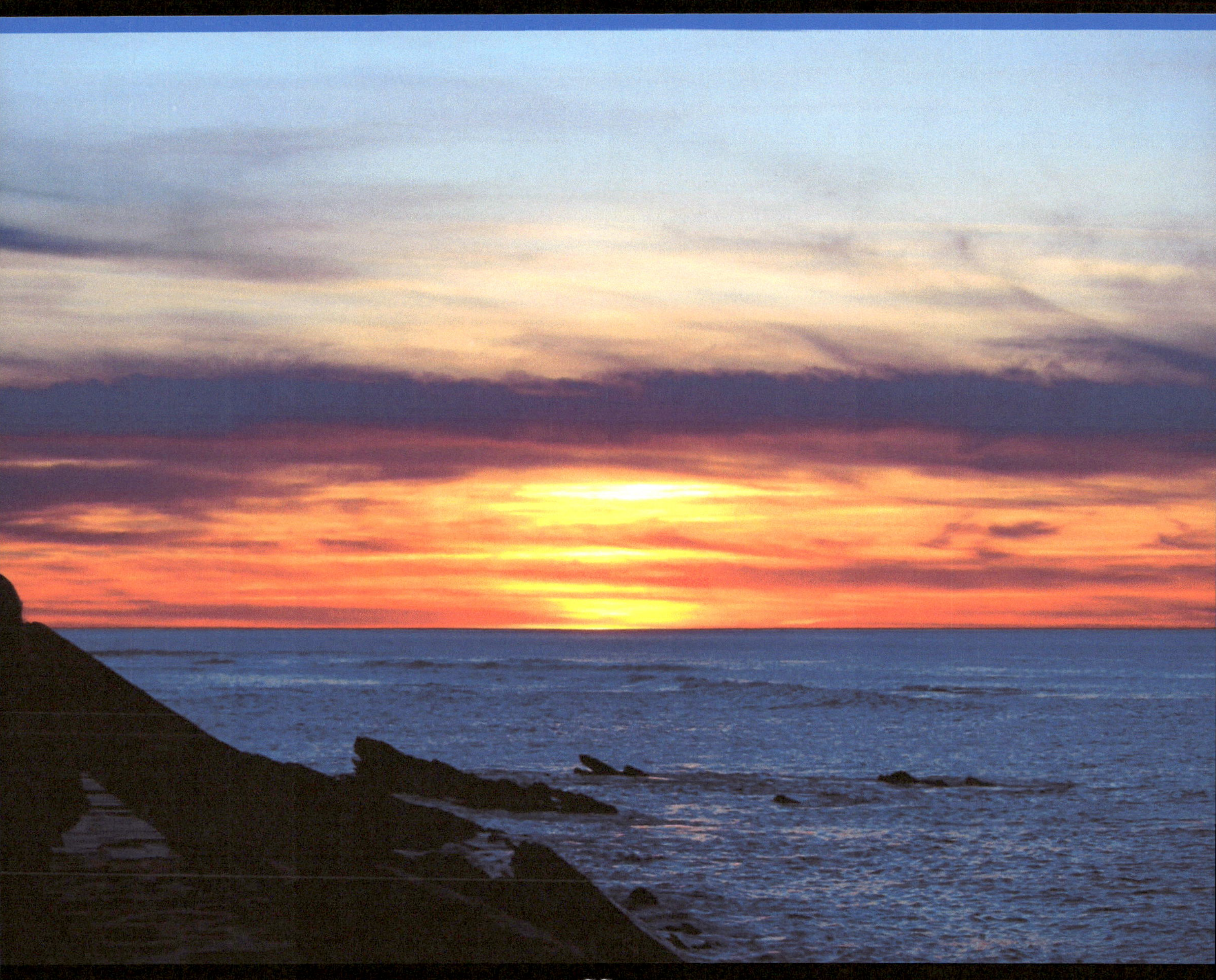

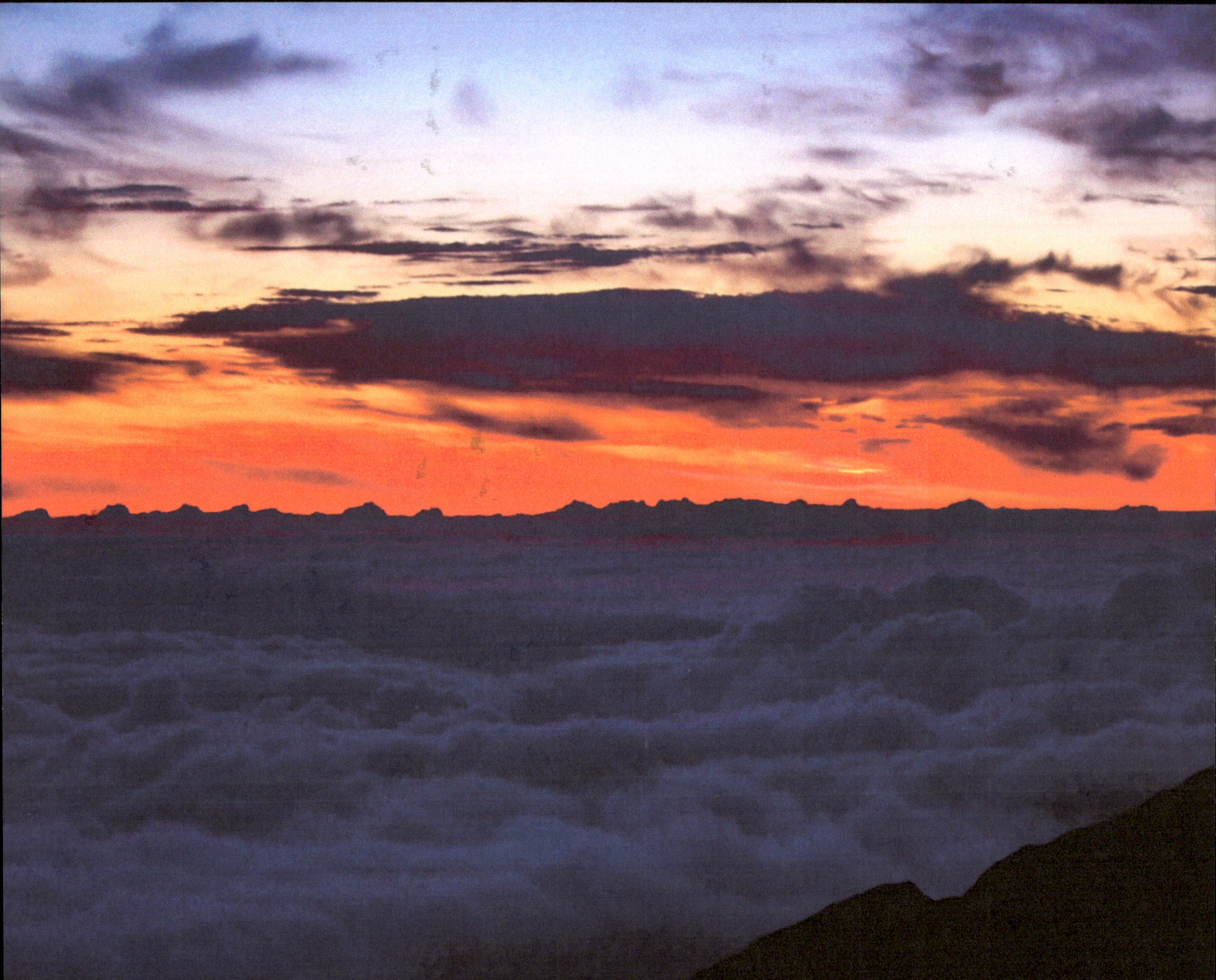

See the majesty before you... How the light lingers in your eyes. You are here to witness the glory; thank heaven that you are alive. You can climb a mountain on courage, truth, and faith, and gather the fruits of your labor to savor on a rainy day. Behold the beauty and vastness of this place. All around you is stillness, perfection, and peace. How lucky you are to be witness paradise here on earth...

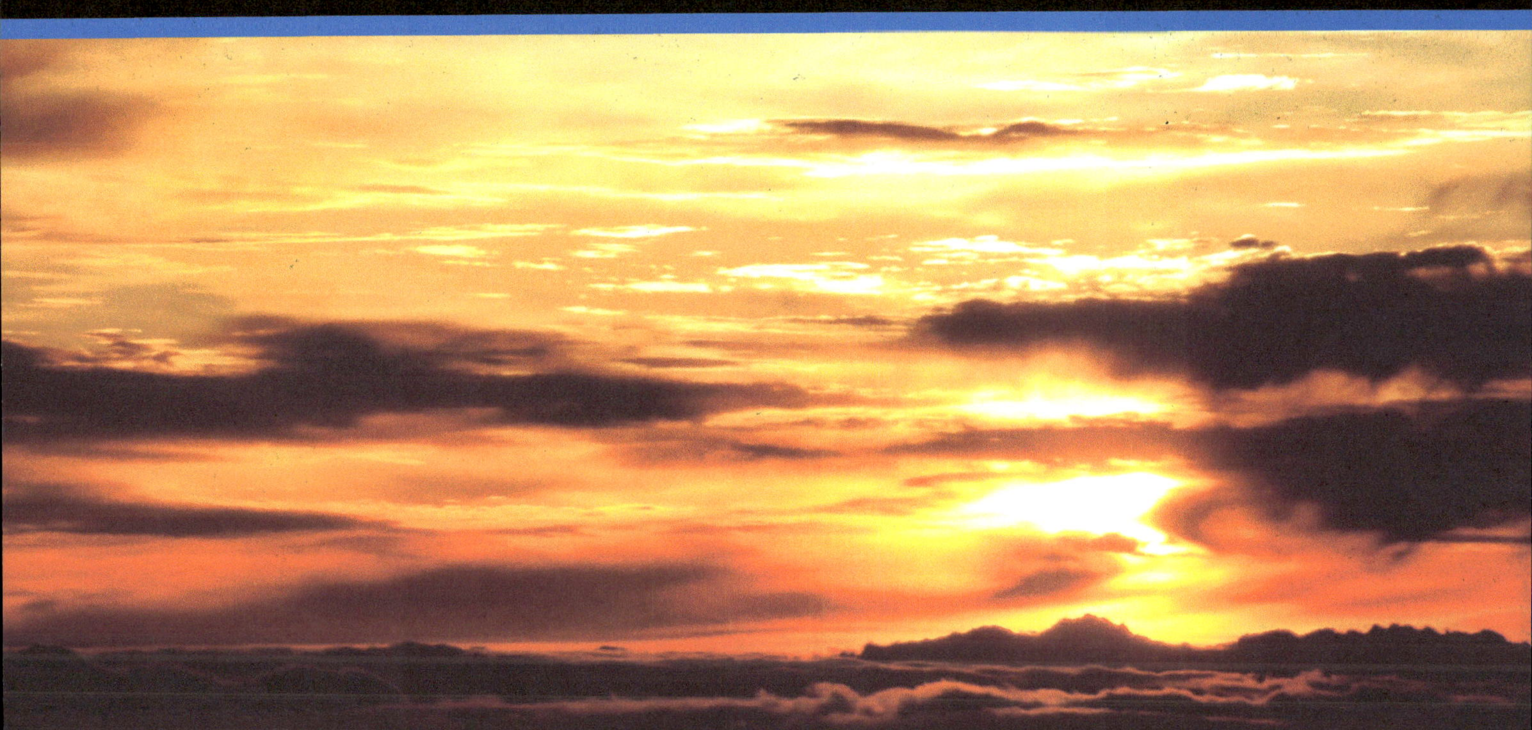

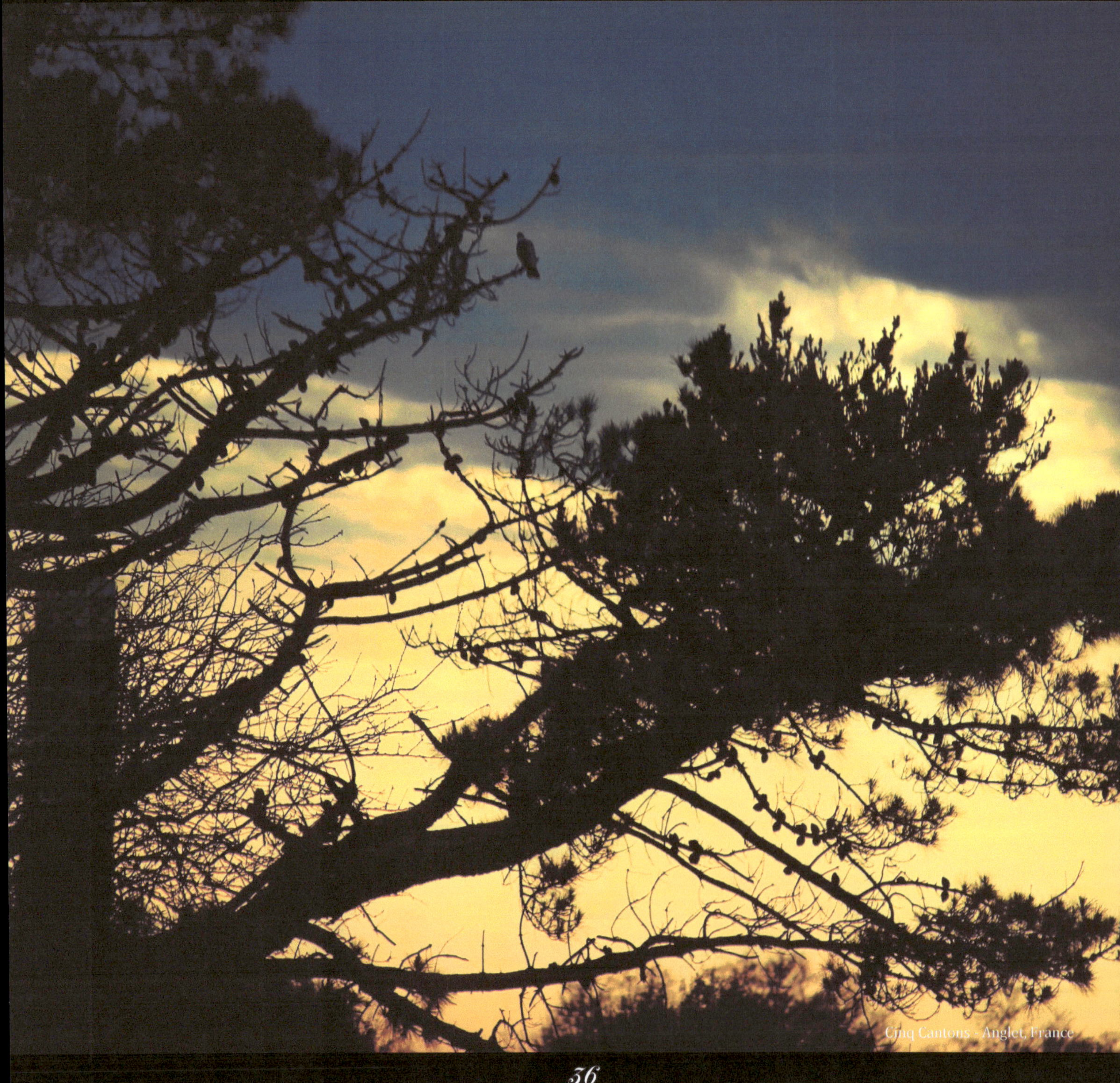

Cinq Cantons - Anglet, France

Beyond yonder hills I mourn, the last golden rays of today's dying sun. And with it's rebirth tomorrow I pray, the end of winter, pain ,and sorrow. For a new time has just begun and with it comes the rising sun. The painful past is already done, so we can begin again and never mourn... We breathe again and therefore we are blessed, for each day we rise, we are reborn, and so is our chance...

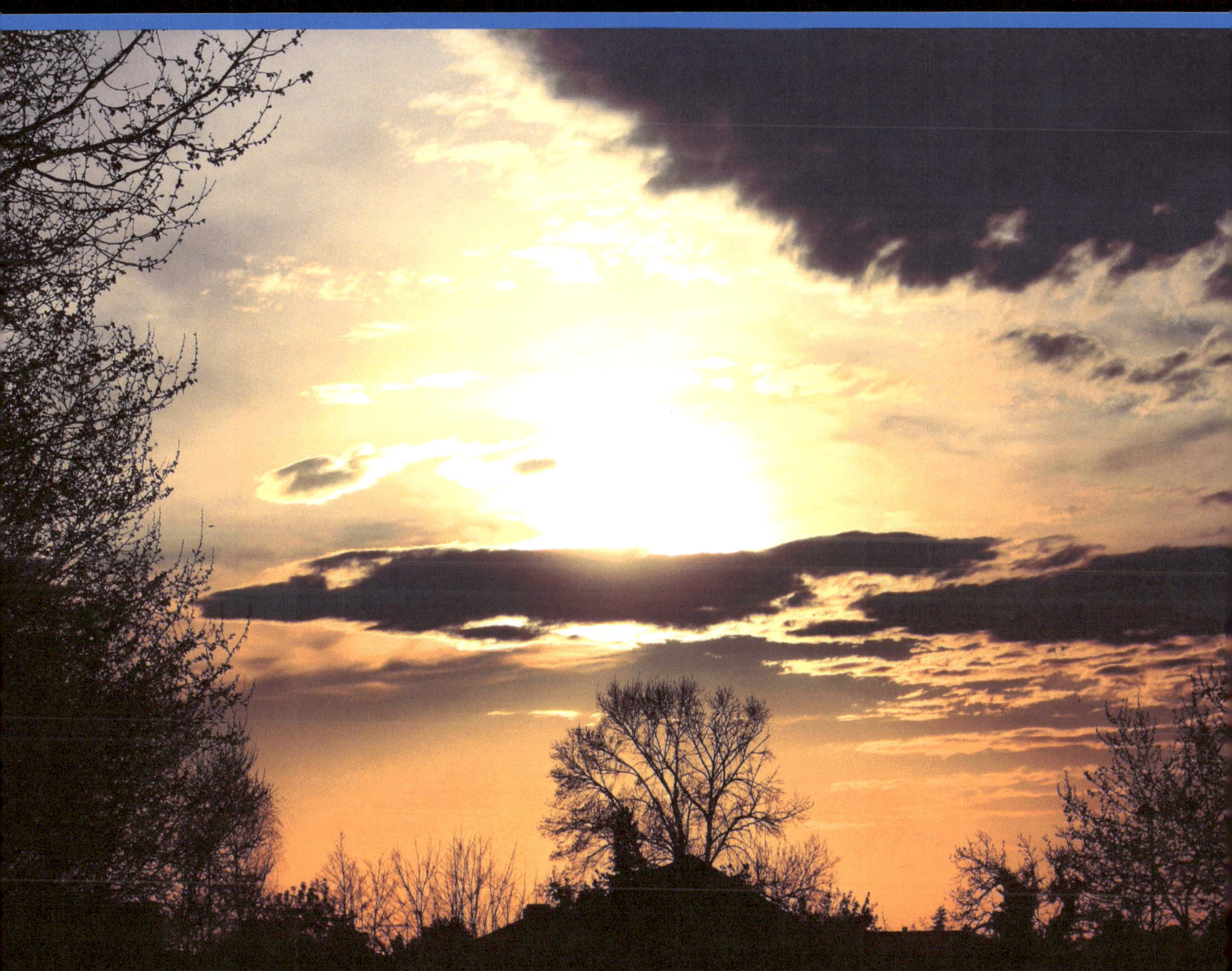

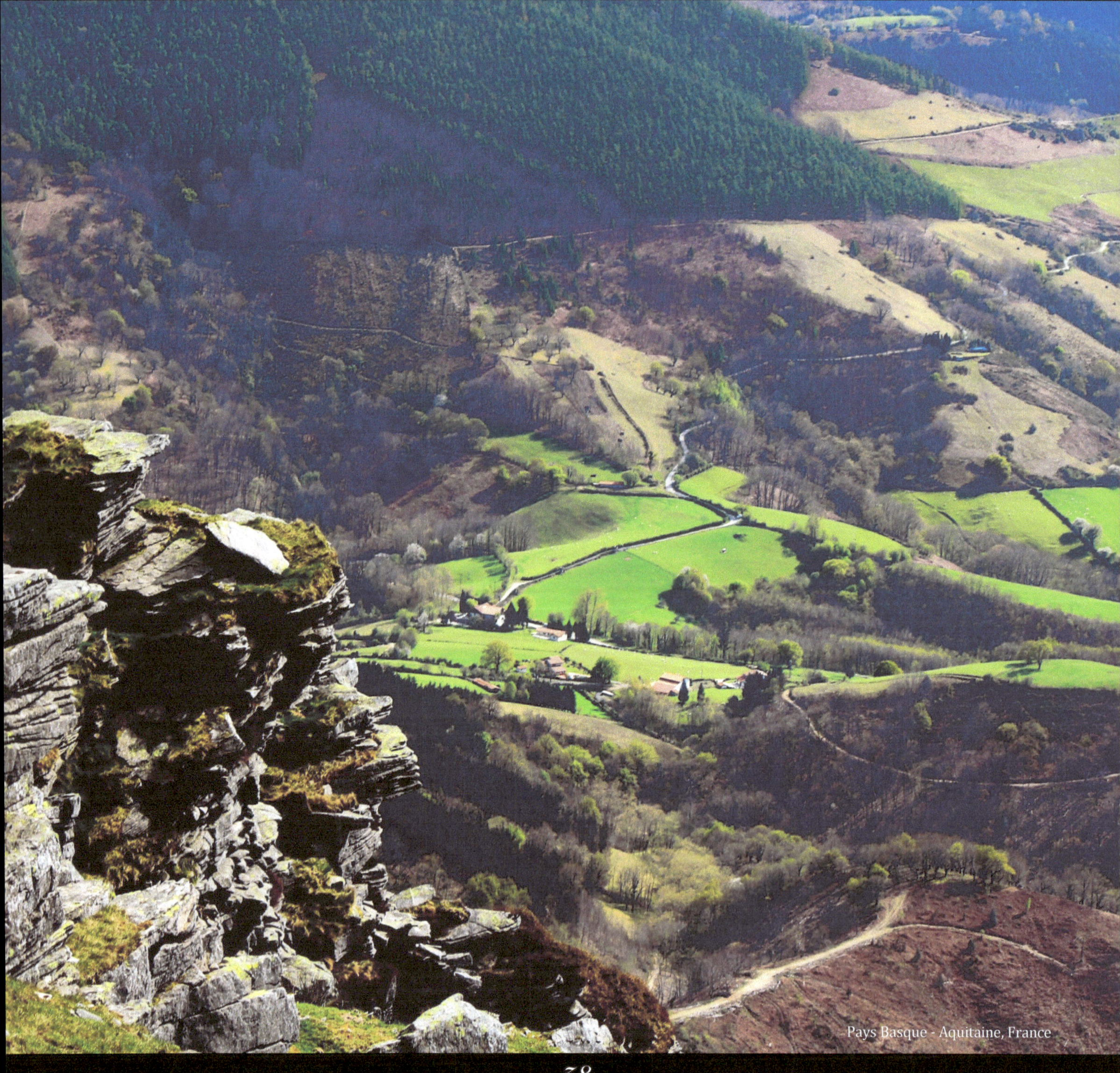

Pays Basque - Aquitaine, France

Life is like a river rushing through your veins; bold and triumphant, fragile, and humane. Mind, body, and spirit all making haste, wielding their desires towards what they wish to taste. The urge of devotion, joy in your heart to hold, the angst when you can't seize what has captured your soul. Life is a victory that you've already won. Claim it today; for today, it is yours...

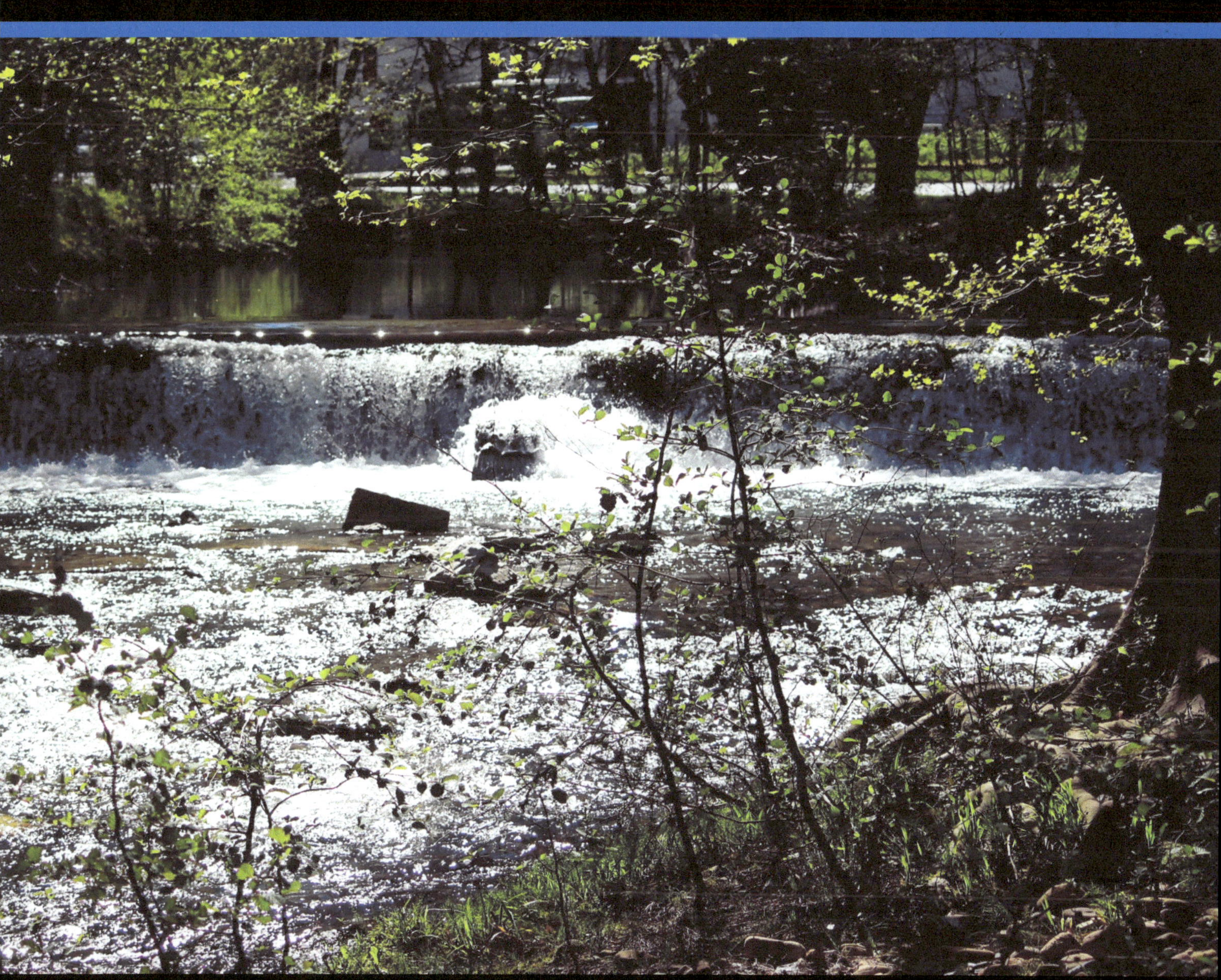

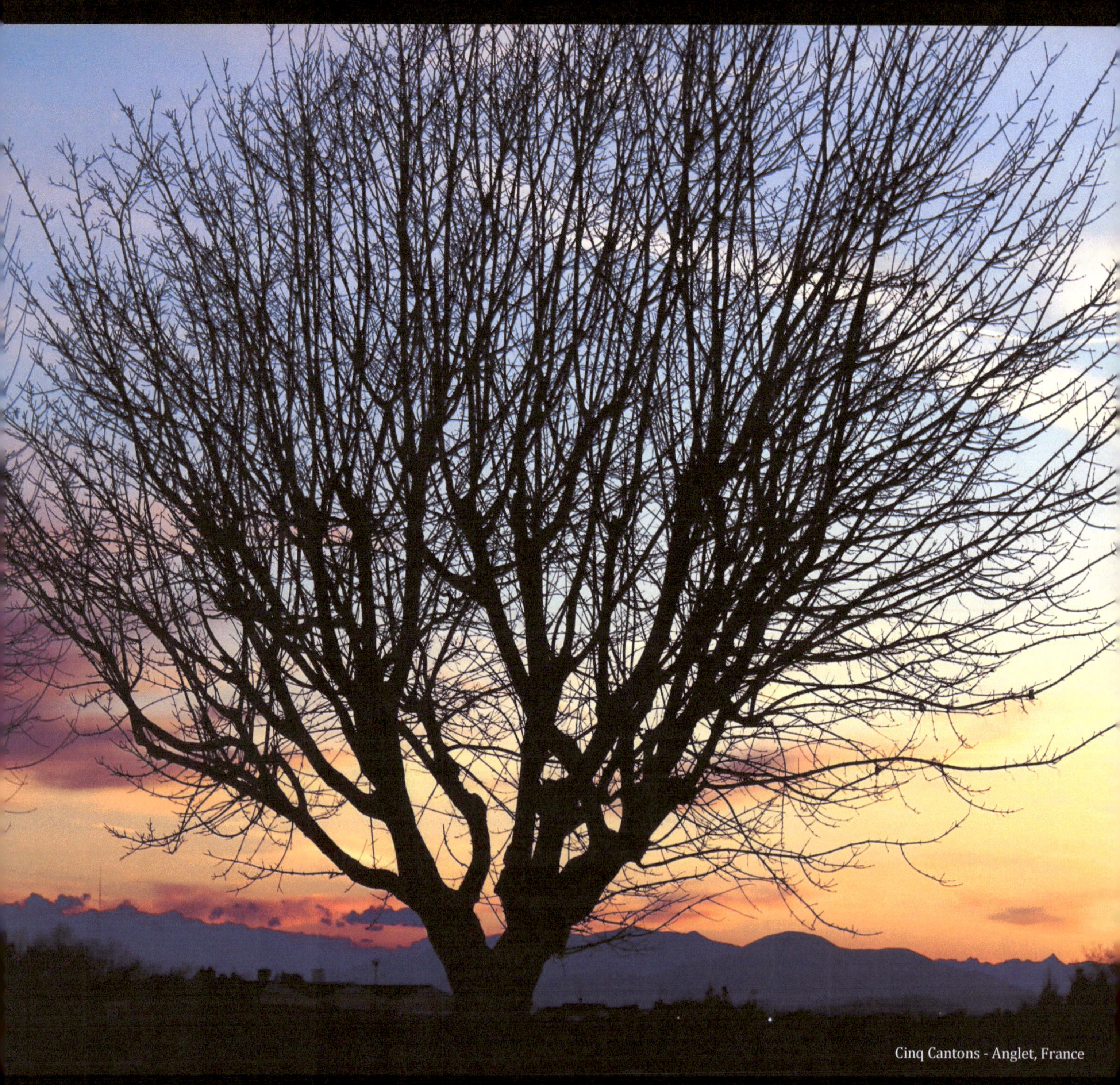
Cinq Cantons - Anglet, France

A shining light in the dark; night didn't prevail. Day comes again bringing the promise of wonders to come. The morning welcomes you with it's fiery show. It's beautiful and lovely; heaven's gift wrapped in a dawn's afterglow. Time to awaken; the winds are howling through the trees. Rise up singing and plant your feet firmly on solid stardust and dreams, for now it is your work that begins.

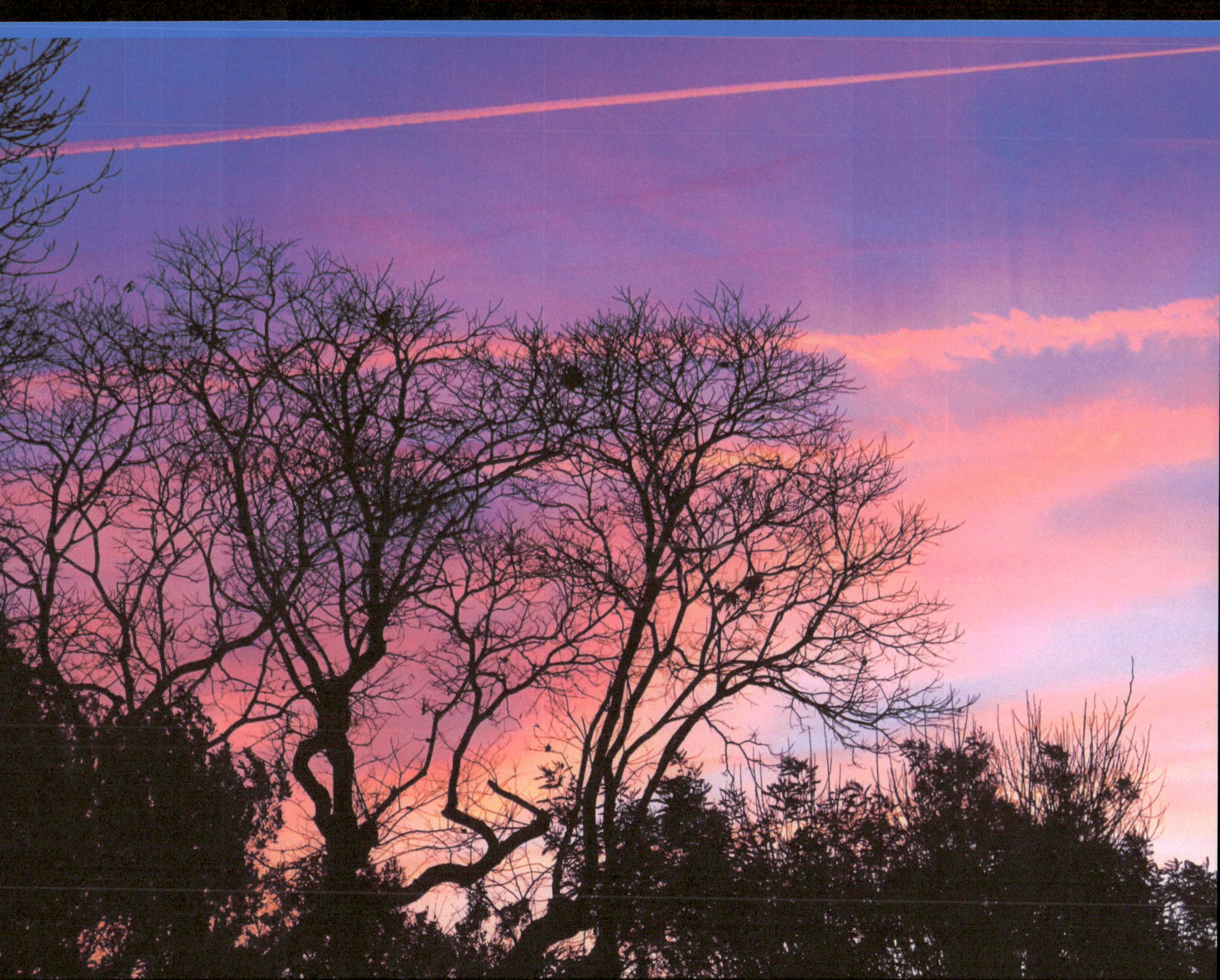

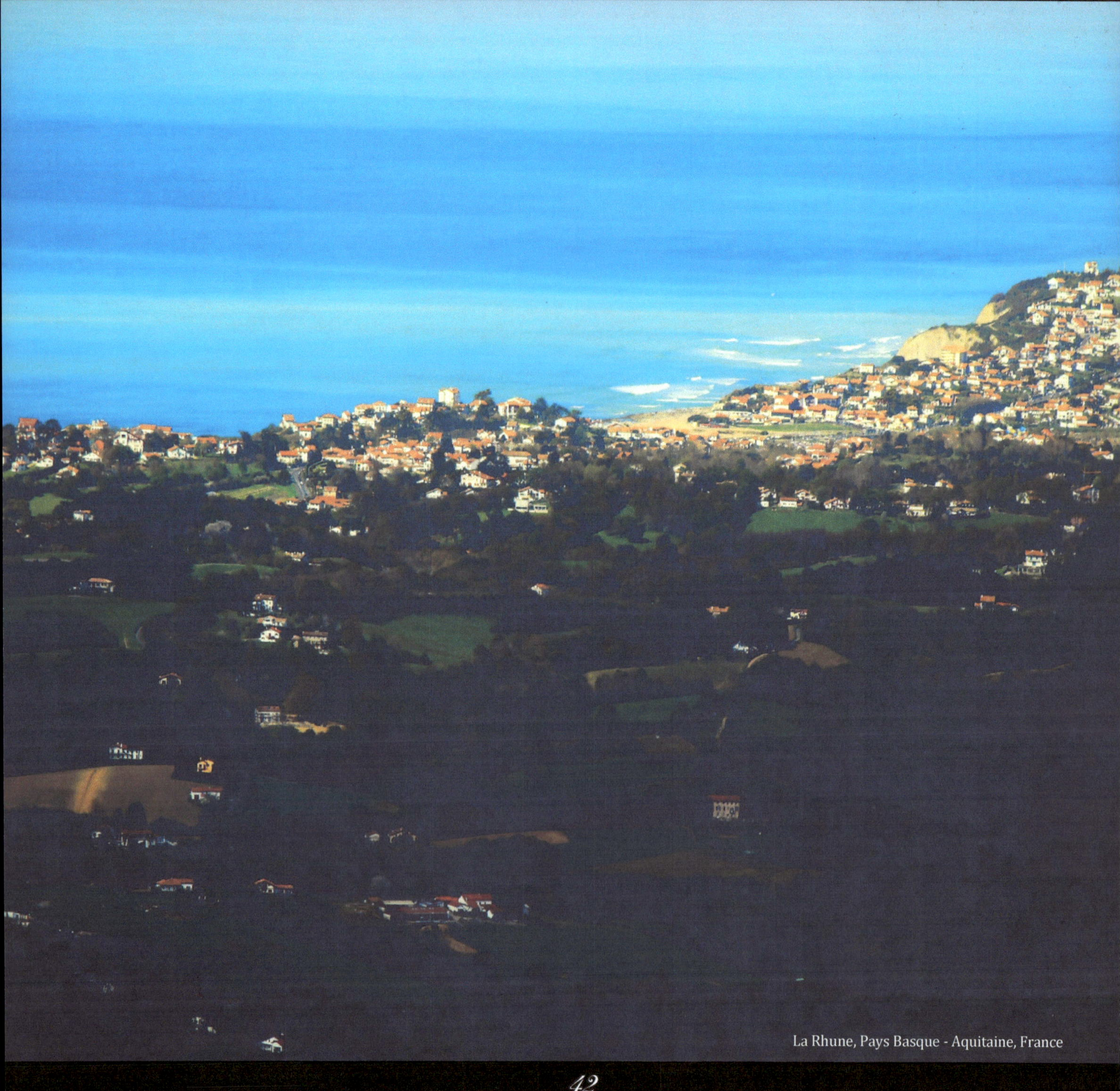

La Rhune, Pays Basque - Aquitaine, France

I stand on faith and the promise of tomorrow. I stand on hope and fiercely fight against sorrow. I stand on love and embrace my the beauty of my dreams. I stand on the courage and always say what I mean. I stand on the law and I stand on truth. I stand for the right to be me and for you to be you. I stand on the shoulders of all who came before. I stand on the sacred mountain and not the shore.

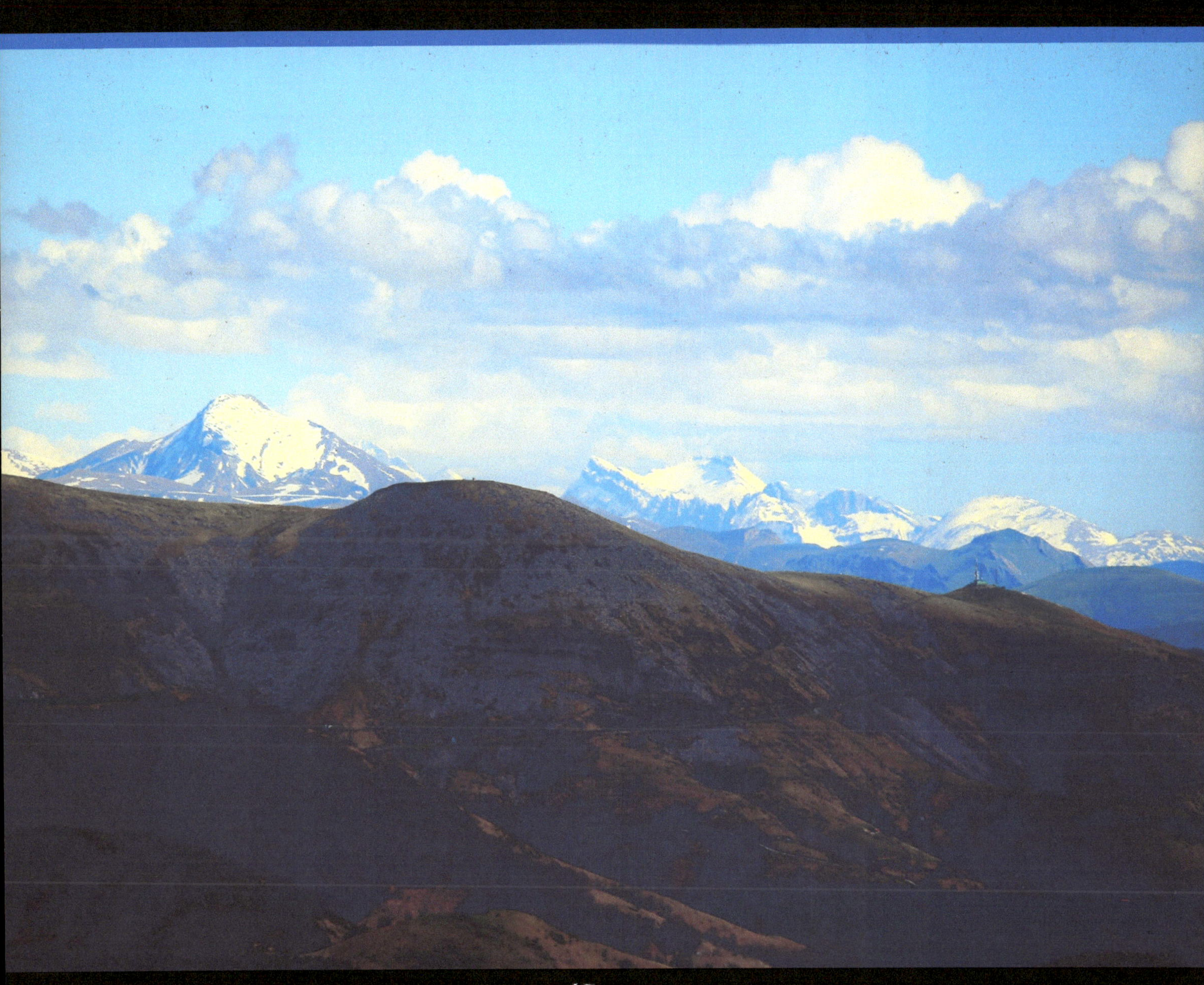

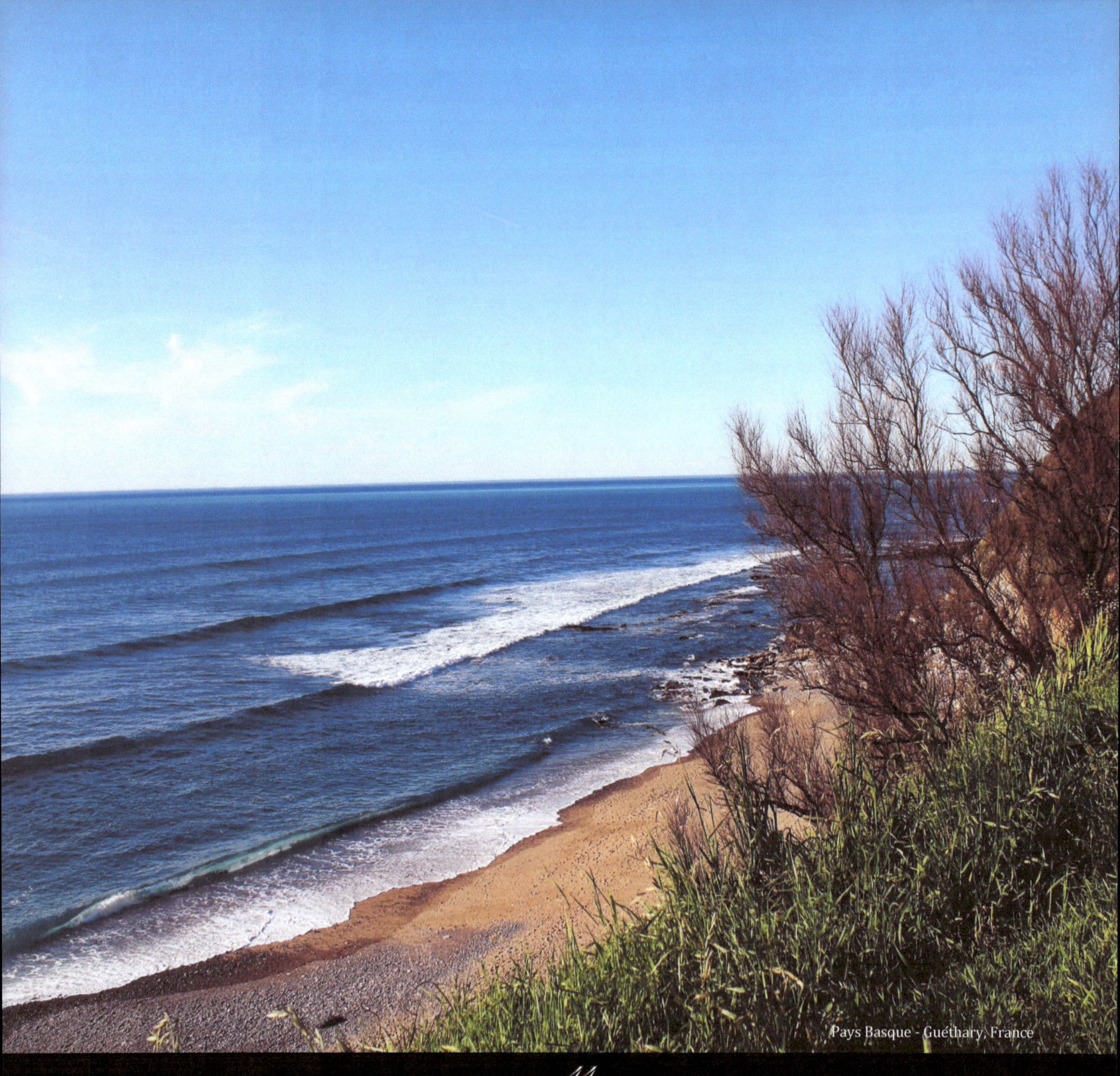

Pays Basque - Guéthary, France

Lift your eyes to glory of heaven, for you bear witness to a day being born. Life is just beginning for some, yet for others we mourn. Be grateful for this moment, for you can begin again. Whatever race you didn't finish, you can now finally win. Heaven is waiting patiently; so there is never a rush to reach the end. Be at peace on your journey, and just breathe... Breathe it all in...

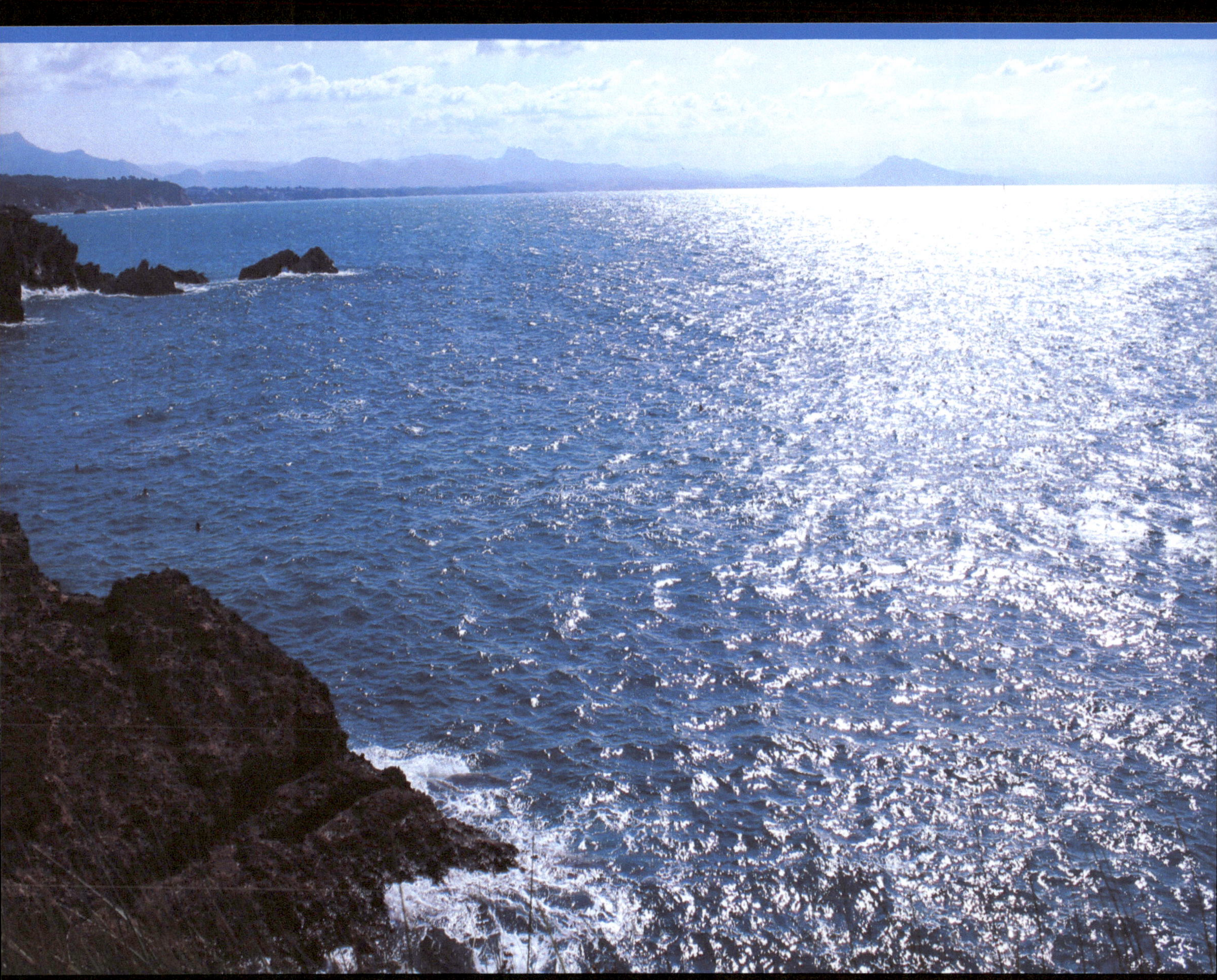

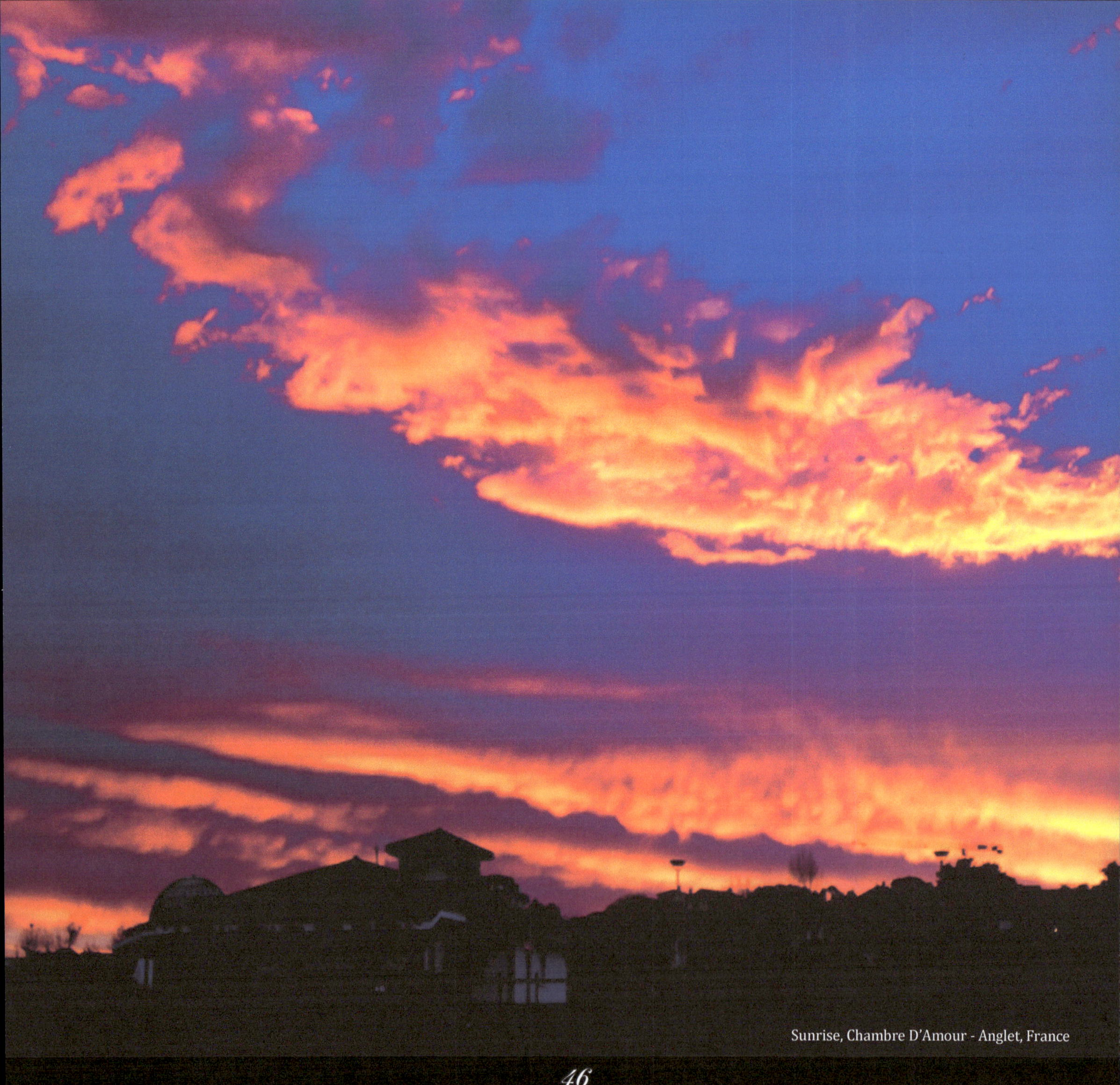
Sunrise, Chambre D'Amour - Anglet, France

Like fire in the sky after the winter rain, the sun parades its power and the clouds captures the flames. Vibrant and luxurious, bold, and unafraid, it covers the heavens victoriously; it's valorously brave. The soldier in the sky is full of legends untold, and nothing could be more breathtaking or wonderful to behold. Look up and see his triumph; he amazes on high... His soul has reached glory in paradise...

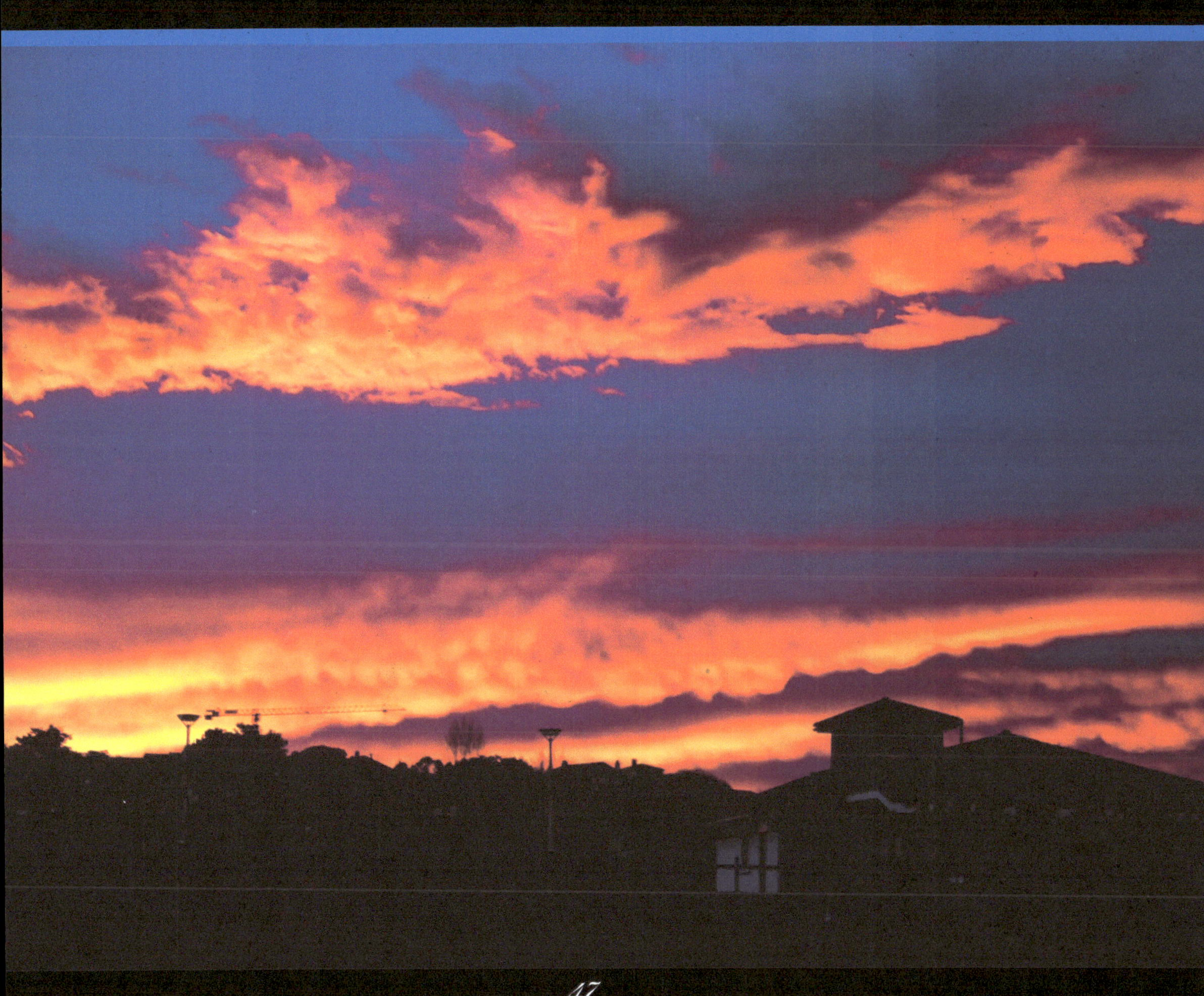

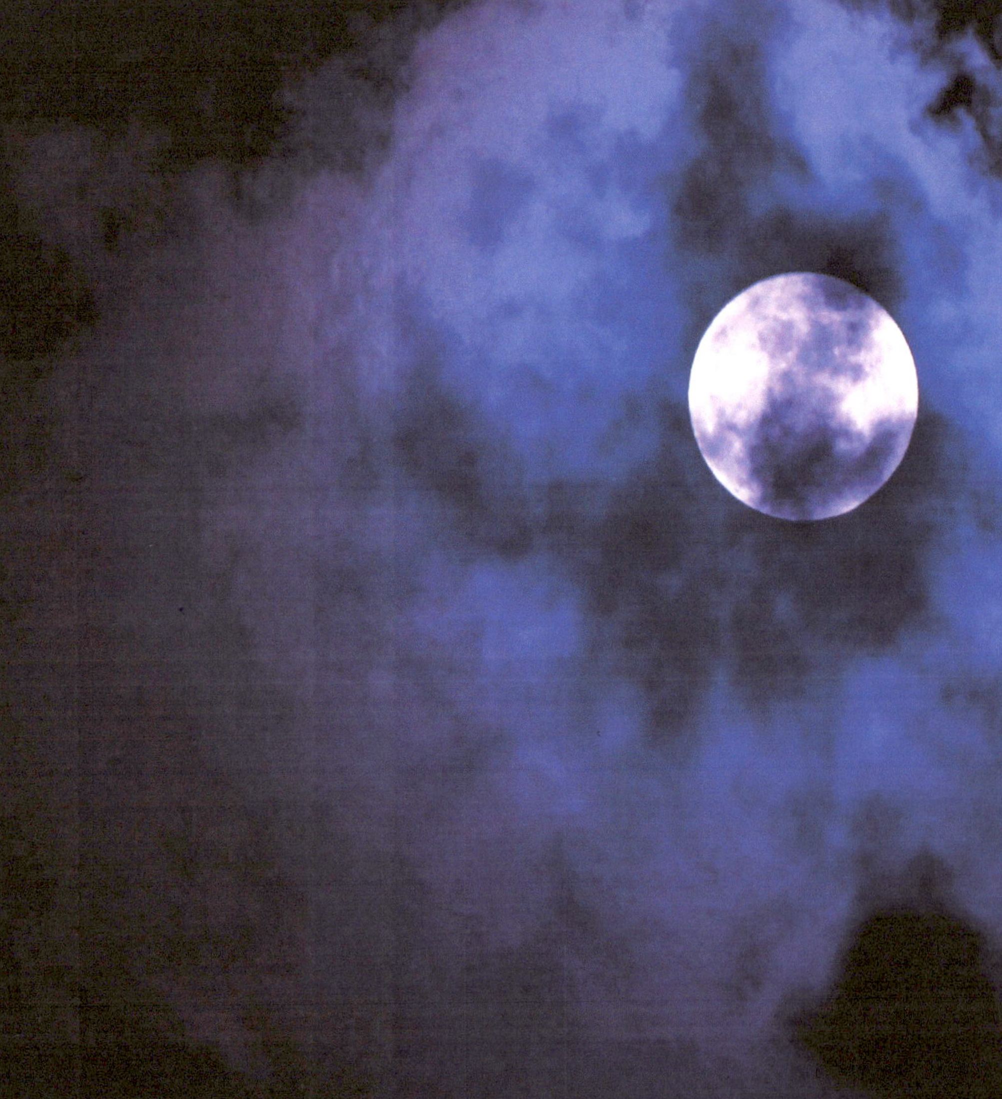

Kihei - Maui, Hawai'i

My emotions runs wild and my spirit runs free. I howl to the moon, "I am free! I am free!" Then to my surprise the word, "Free!" returns to me. "I made it!" I shout loudly, "How can that be?". Then I hear, "Made it!" suddenly shouting back at me. I lift my head and clap my hands. "Thank you!" I cry to heaven and "No, thank you..." softly answers me. Life is your echo...watch and see.

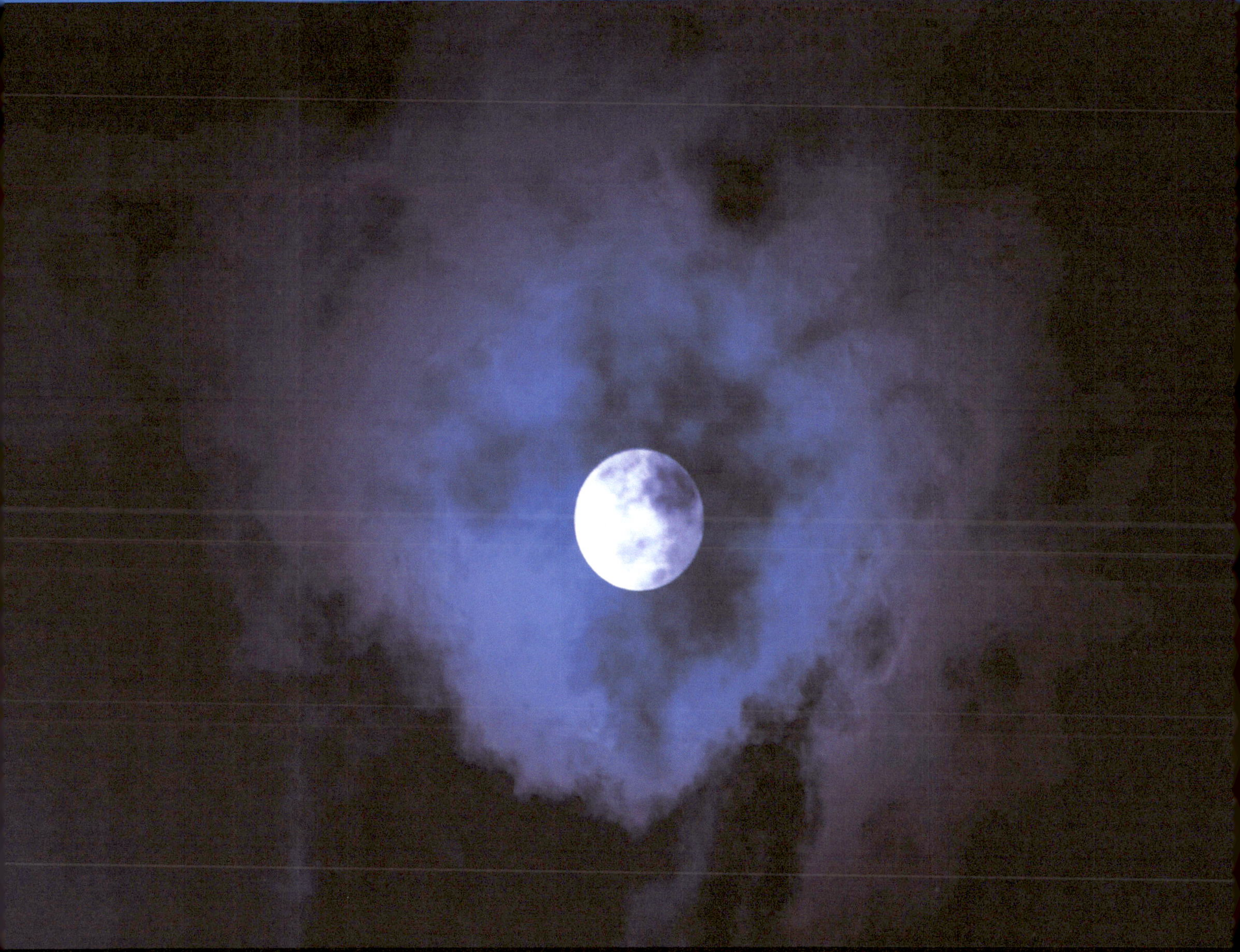

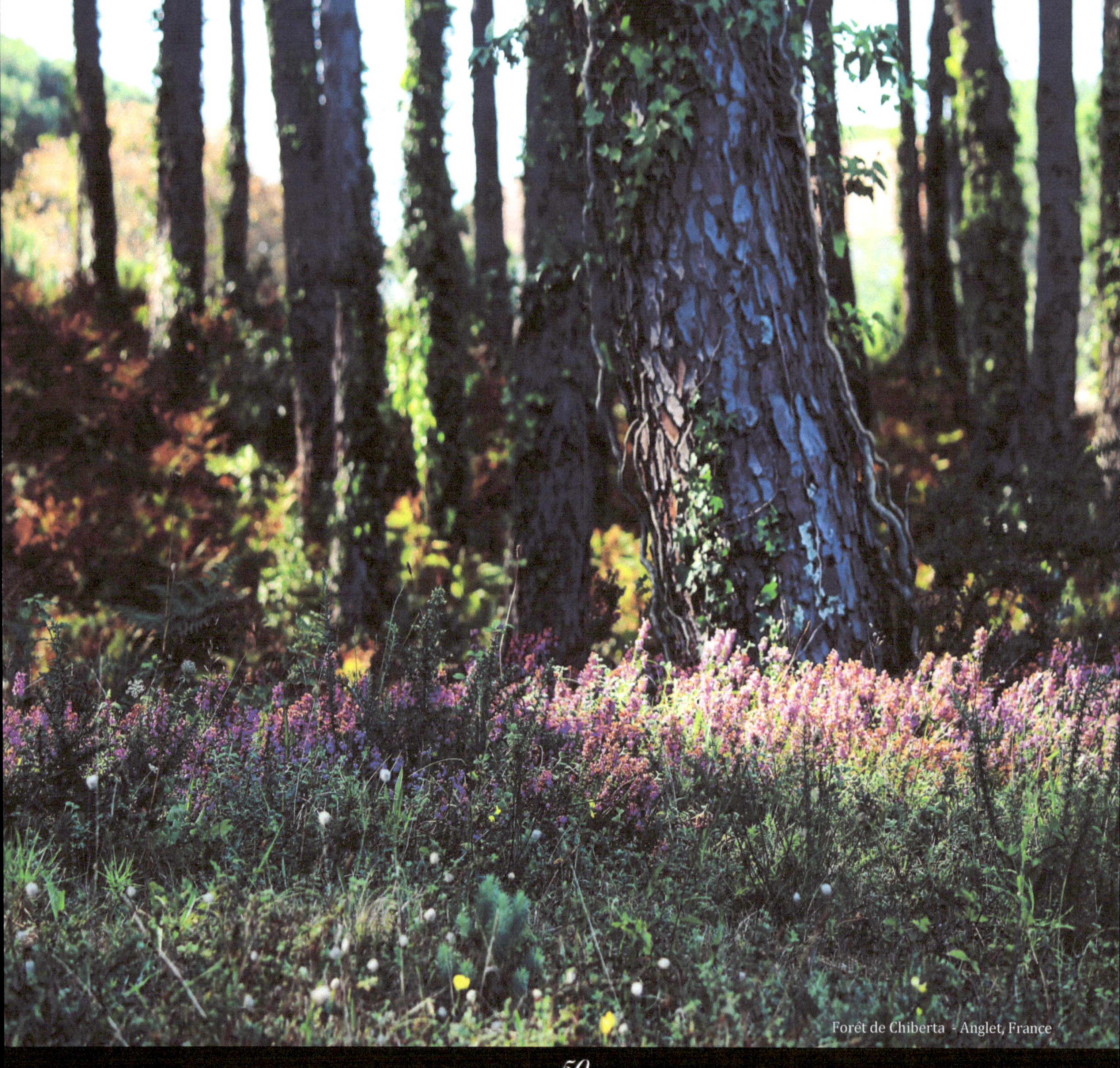

Forêt de Chiberta - Anglet, France

The path once traveled is far behind me now, as I move upward toward the light. The painful past, the bane of my existence, is no longer my reason to cry. It has become a lush and fragrant meadow nourished by the tears I cried for I have traveled far on this journey. I have endured a tragic beginning, but gave it all to reach the end. Now, I are here; the worst is over and it will never be again...

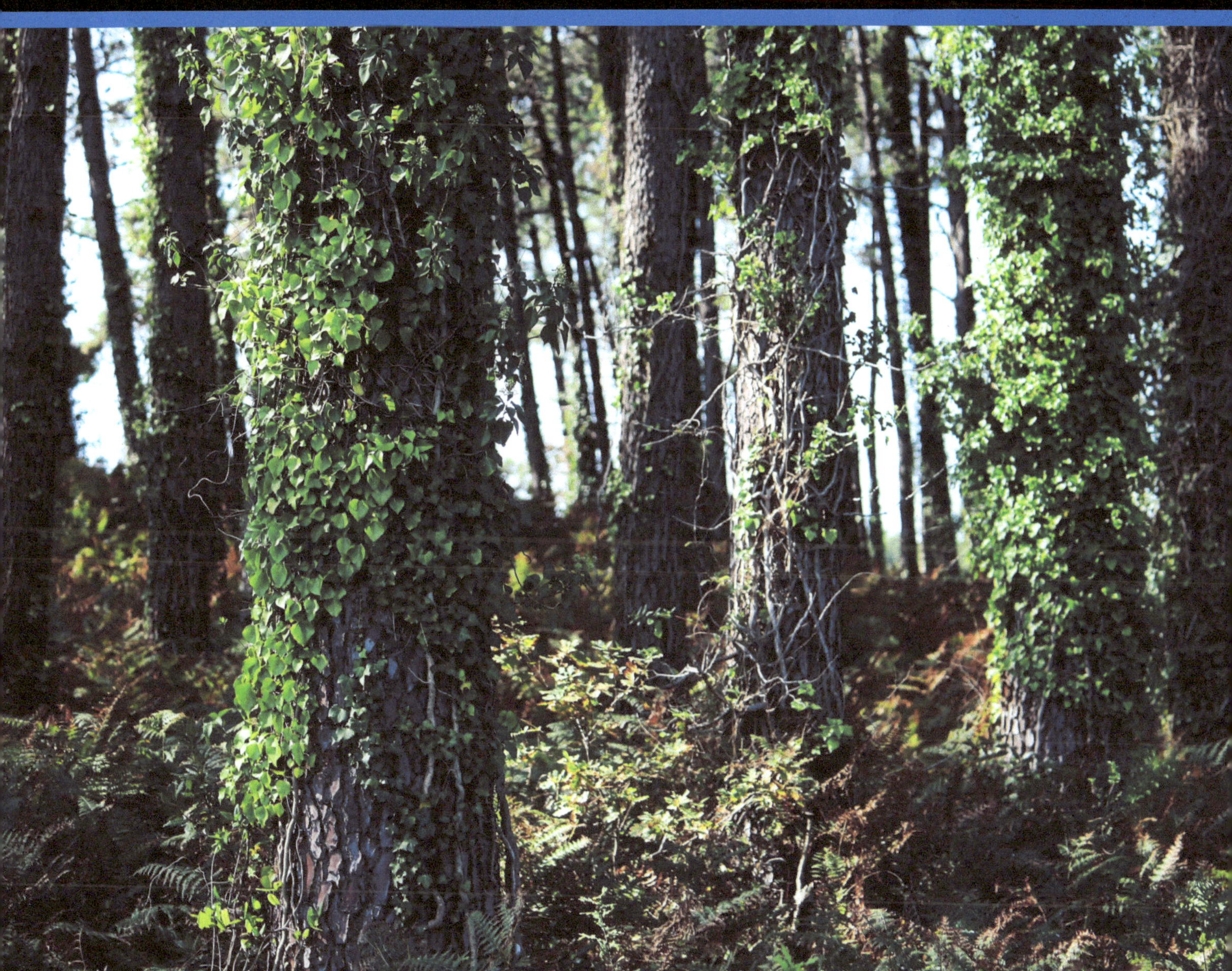

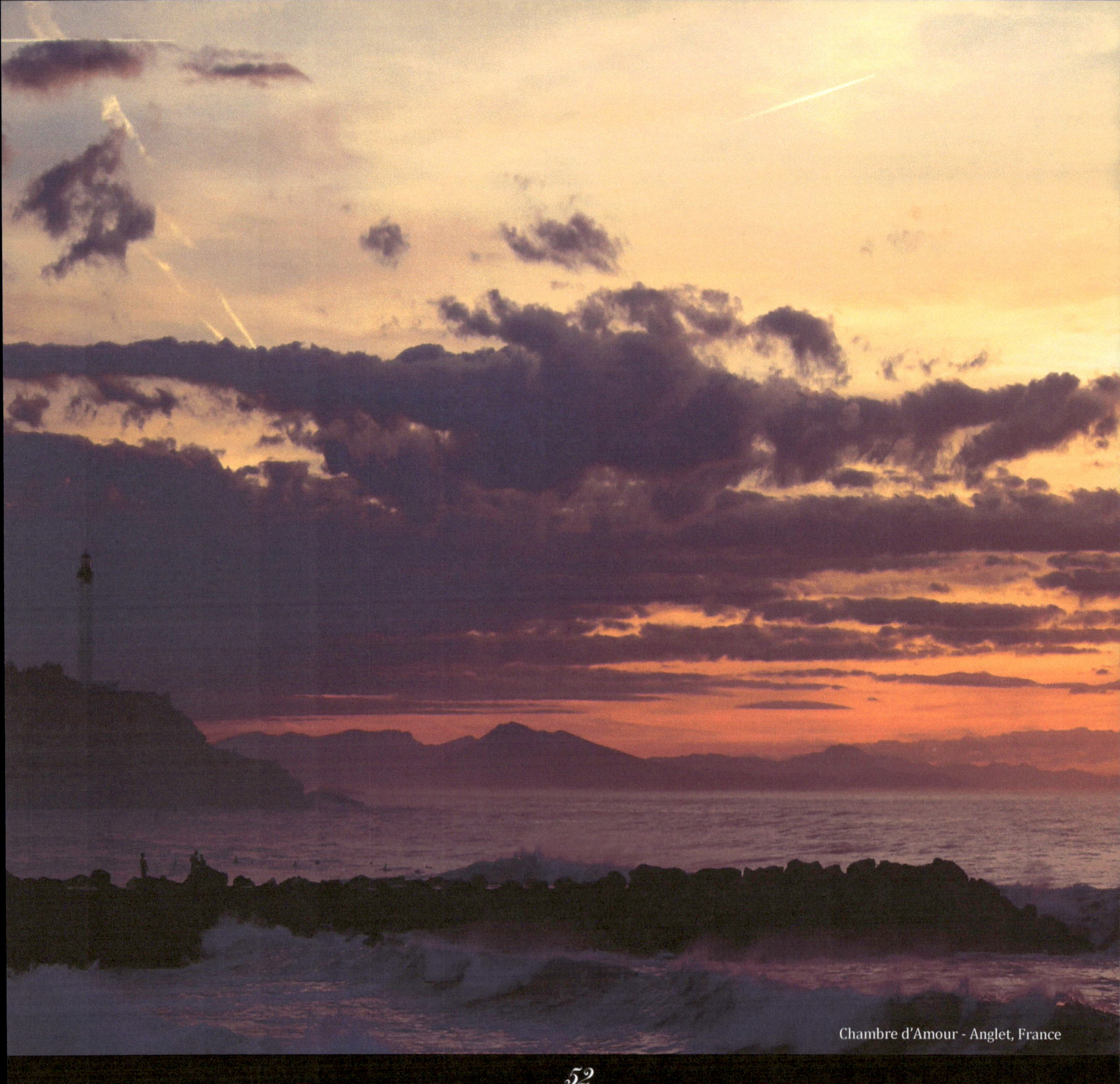

Chambre d'Amour - Anglet, France

Gaze at the setting sun and rejoice, for you are alive. There is a purpose to your journey, and a reason you have survived. You may have cursed your trepid journey with every step you took and ignored the precious moments, and crushed them underfoot. But now see your victory in your struggle to survive, for when the sun goes down, you were there to see it smile, and you'll be here when it arise...

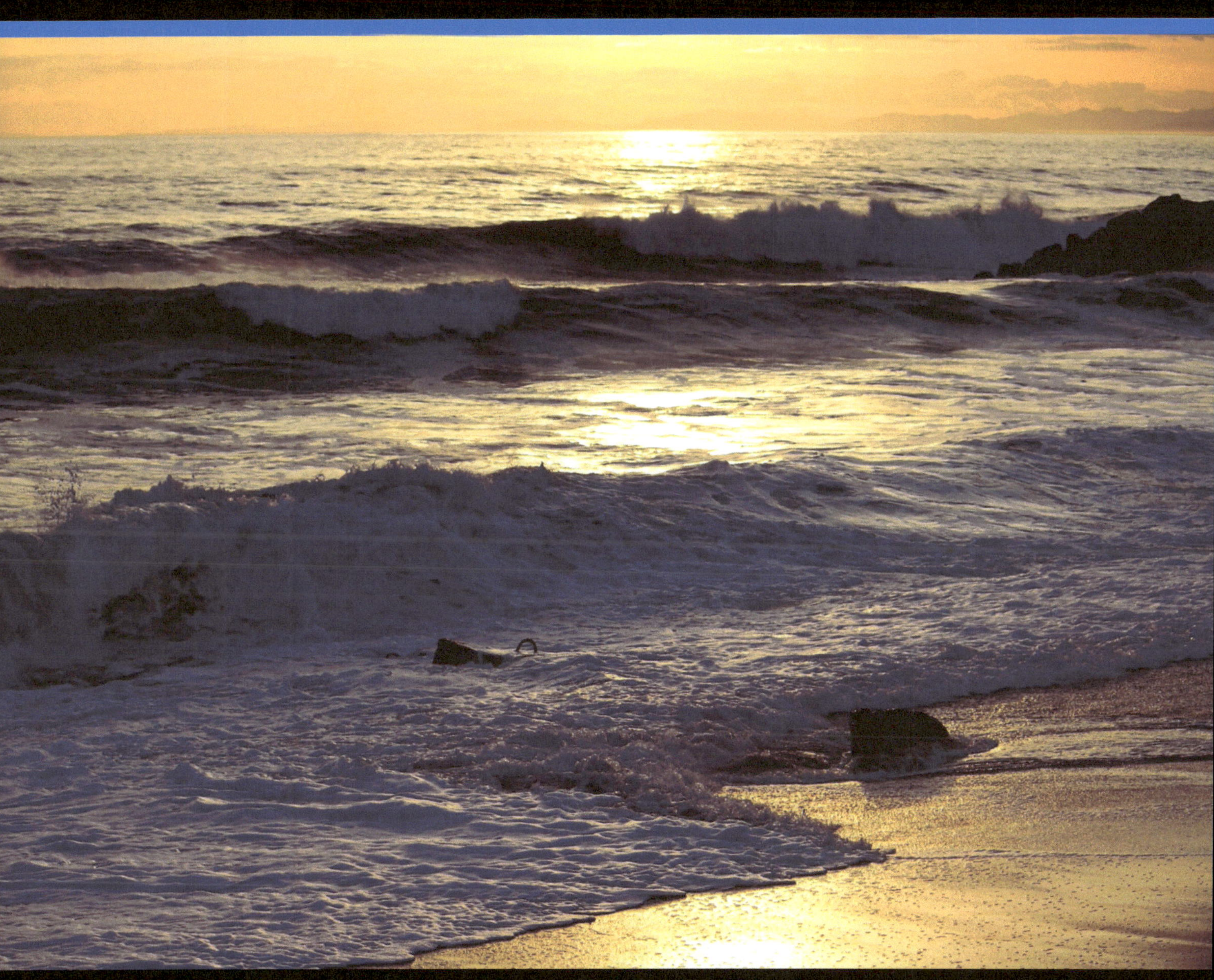

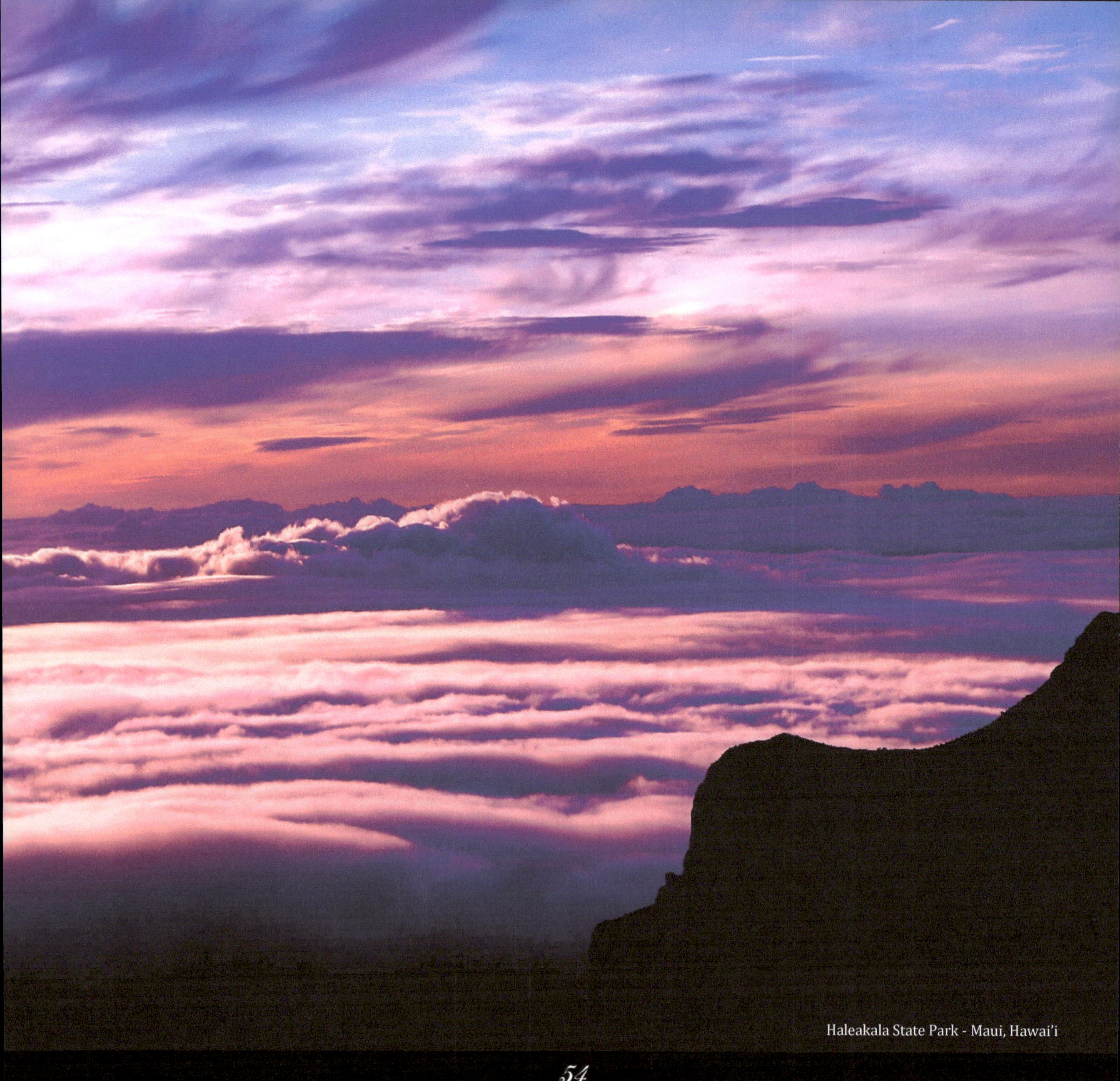

Haleakala State Park - Maui, Hawai'i

Stand tall on the mountain. This all belongs to you. It is your kingdom, for you are the ruler this world. Look out over the horizon and all the glory it beholds. Live triumphant and feel secure. You have nothing to be afraid of... You are the heir of something marvelously magnificent, for this earth was gifted to you. You are the mountain, you are the planet, for you are the child of God...

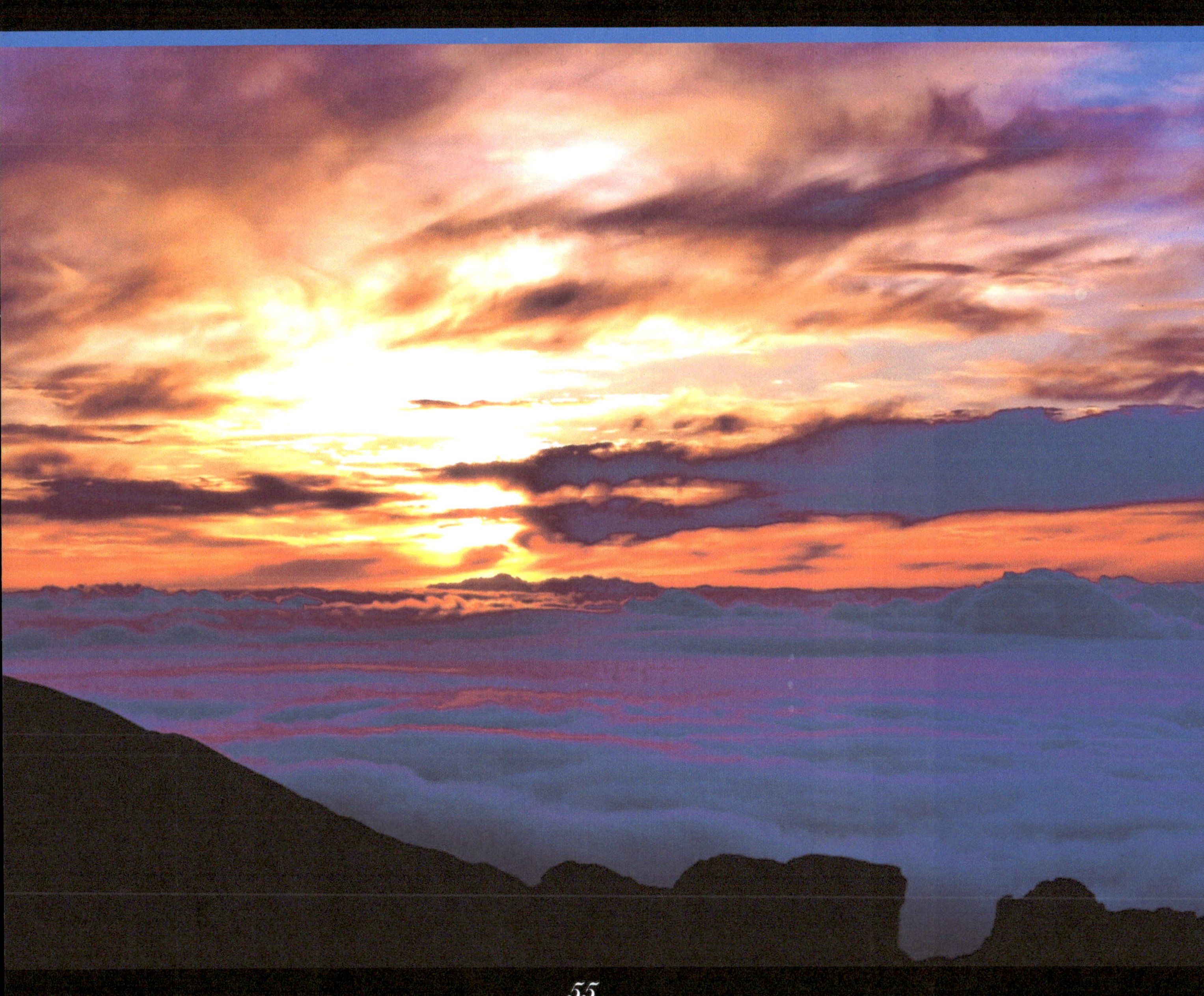

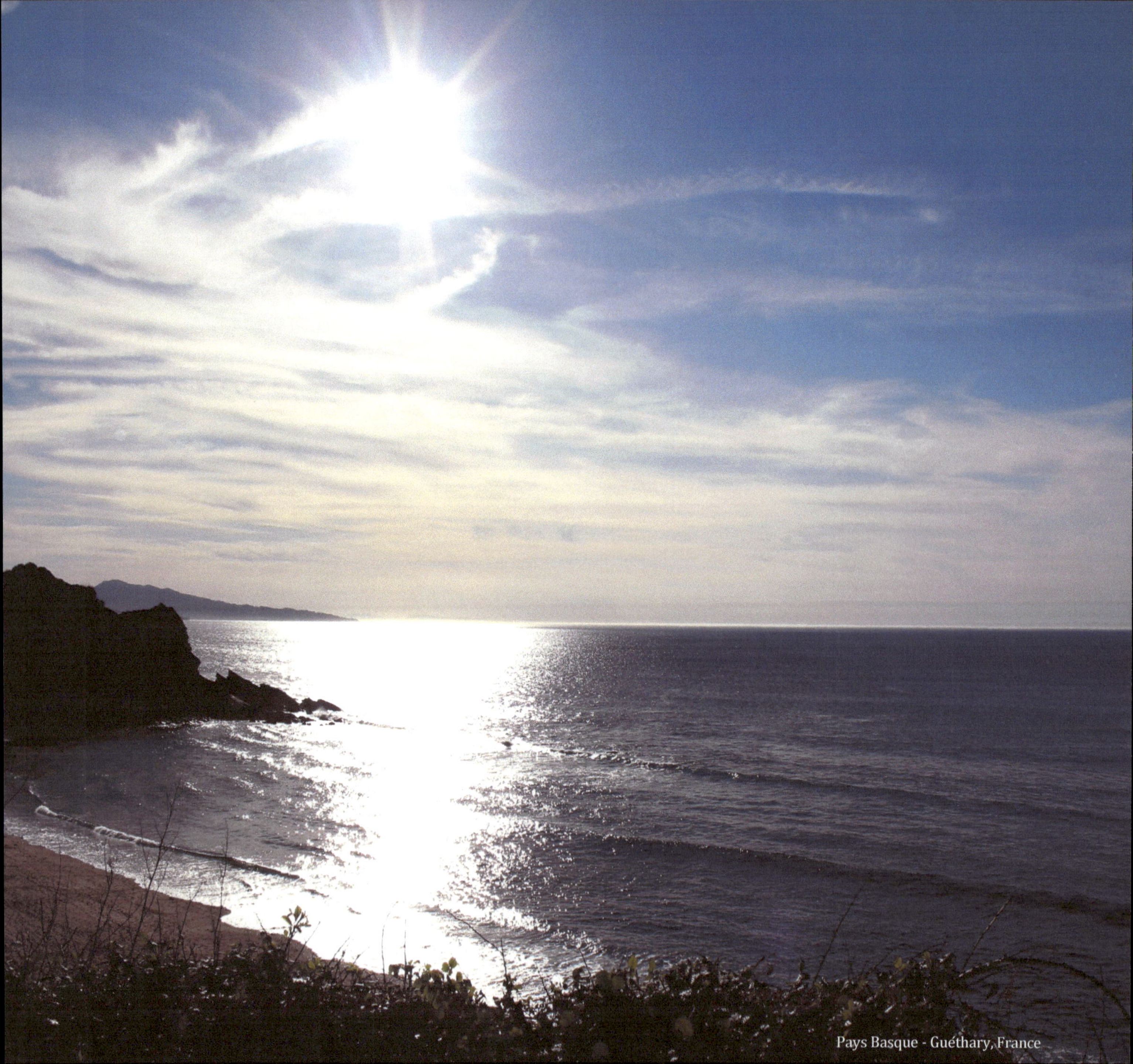
Pays Basque - Guéthary, France

May perfect peace wash over the earth like forgiving loving grace. It feels like being sanctified with the sun on your face. When love touches you like sparkling rays on the sea, fear, anger, and guilt sweetly disappears. And heaven's kisses of waterfalls cleanse your pain away. It is a wondrous day of your journey and the best moment to pray, for between heaven and earth is where we live until we die...

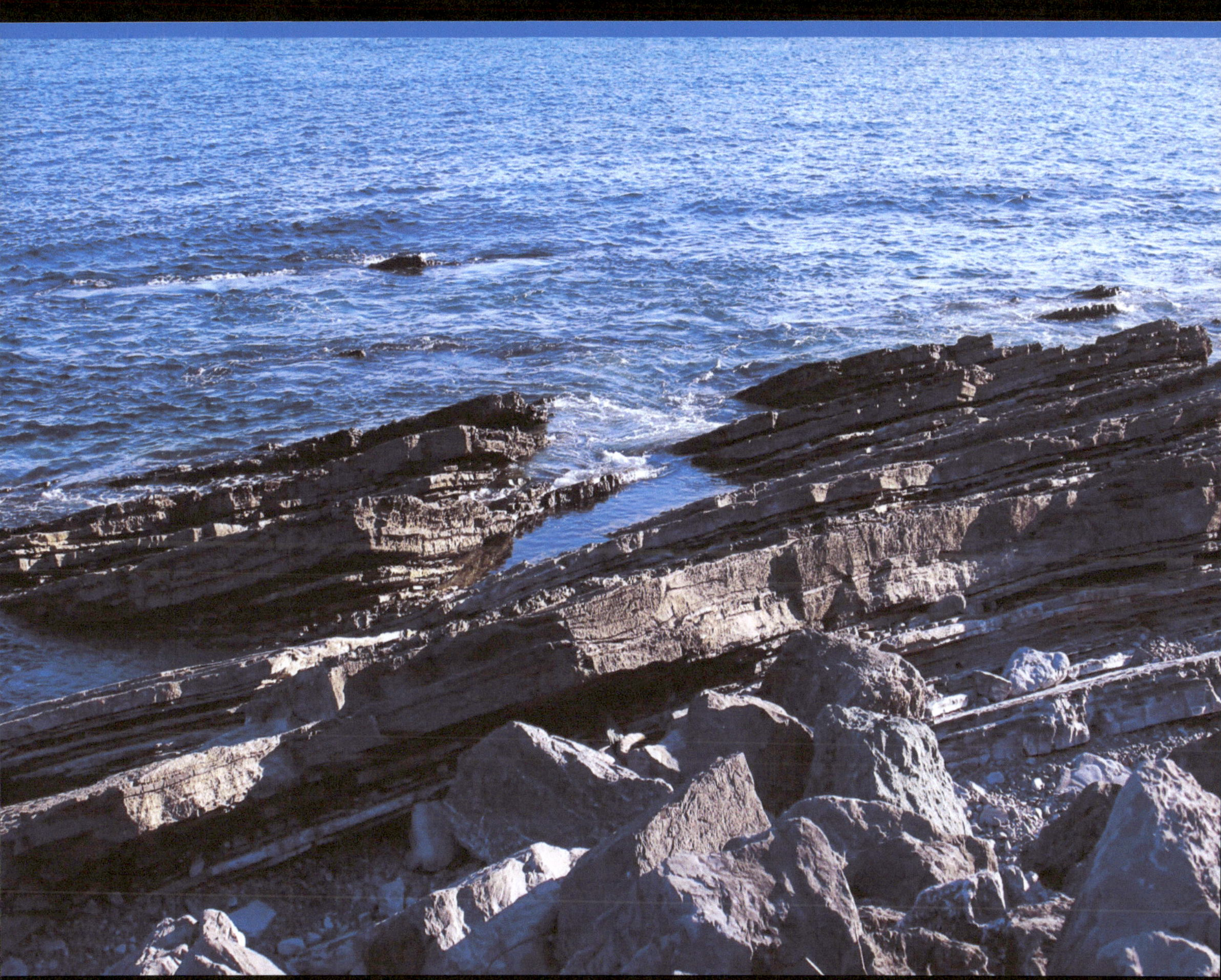

If I can inspire a heart to beat again, or breathe life into a dream;
hearten those who cry in the night and bring them the morning sun,
then my journey was worth the tears, and I triumphed in the midst of them all.

-D. Ashanti-Dubois

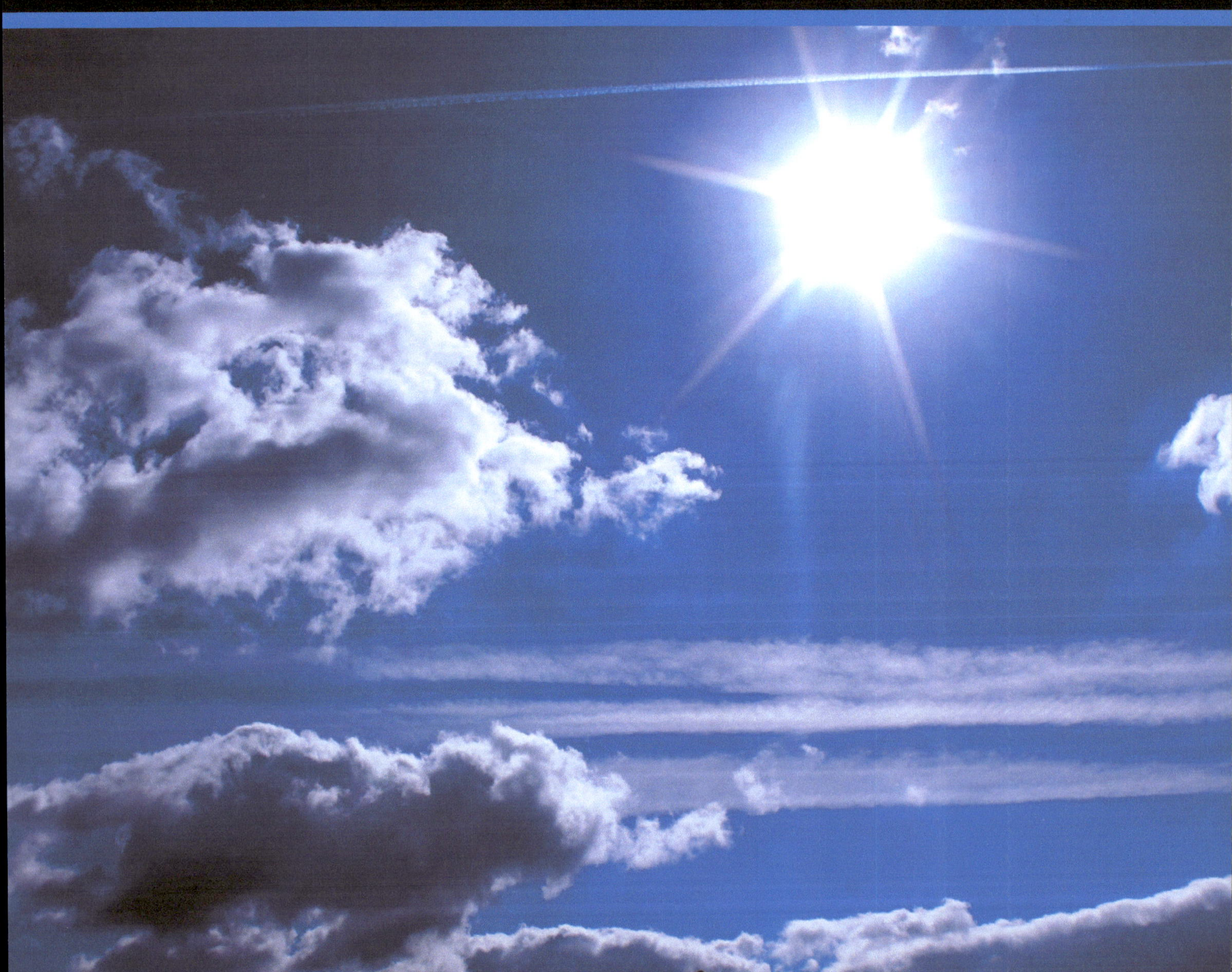

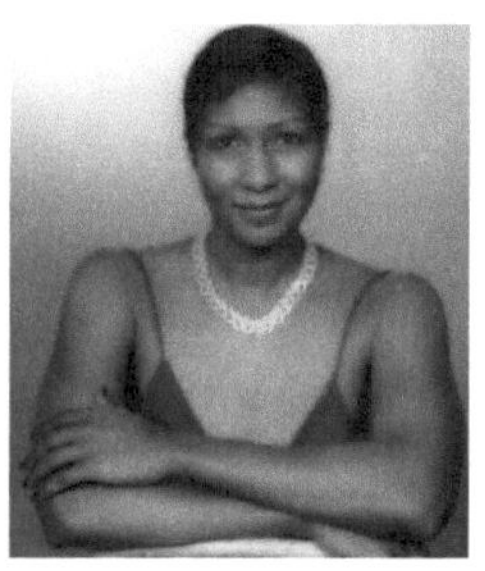

ABOUT THE AUTHOR

Author and creative artist D. Ashanti-Dubois brings light and love to the universe of literature through her latest edition, Heaven & Earth – Paradise Et La Terre. As a multifaceted writer, photographer, vocalist, composer, graphiste, and artiste, D. Ashanti-Dubois brings a unique perspective to the world of spiritual enlightenment. After nearly two decades of living internationally and in Hawaii, her many travels have emboldened her belief in the spirit of hope, love, and humanity.

Born and raised in St. Louis, Missouri where she began her creative journey writing poetry, prose, and songs at the tender age of five, D. Ashanti-Dubois continues her artistic odyssey producing various genres of books, music, photography, and art. Her spiritual anthology, *Messages of Hope,* is a collection of beautifully written spiritual insights that will inspire and empower your life. The entire Messages of Hope series can be purchased online through Amazon.com and other vendors.

Also available: *Messages of Hope – Words to Uplift the Human Spirit (Special Edition):* An uplifting book of 33 inspire messages and 40 exercises to heal your life with more than 200 gorgeous original photographs. *Messages d'Amour – Reflections of Love:* A romantic diary of love poems with gorgeous floral photography to inspire love and romance. *When You Need A Miracle – Pray:* A magnificent collection of spiritual prayers to uplift the weary heart and nature photography.

For more books available by D. Ashanti-Dubois visit www.mydovesong.com. Look for other editions scheduled to be released in the coming years.

www.ingramcontent.com/pod-product-compliance
Lightning Source LLC
LaVergne TN
LVHW070148110826
845147LV00002B/352

9780692022047